Editor

Erica N. Russikoff, M.A.

Illustrator

Clint McKnight

Cover Artist

Brenda DiAntonis

Editor in Chief

Ina Massler Levin, M.A.

Creative Director

Karen J. Goldfluss, M.S. Ed.

Art Coordinator

Renée Christine Yates

Imaging

Rosa C. See

Publisher

Mary D. Smith, M.S. Ed.

Differentiated Nonfiction Reading

GRADE **3**

- Each passage is written at 3 different levels: easier, average, more challenging
- Content areas include Science, Geography, History, and Language Arts

Teacher Created Resources

Author

Debra J. Housel, M.S. Ed.

Teacher Created Resources, Inc.

12621 Western Avenue
Garden Grove, CA 92841
www.teachercreated.com

ISBN: 978-1-4206-2920-0

©2010 Teacher Created Resources, Inc.

Reprinted, 2020

Made in U.S.A.

Teacher Created Resources

Table of Contents

Introduction

If you are like most teachers, your classroom includes a wide variety of students: average students, English language learners, gifted students, and learning disabled students. You may be expected to get your diverse student population, including special education students and those for whom English is a second language, to master grade-level, content-area material. That's a challenging task and one that requires grade-level, content-area materials written at several levels. *Differentiated Nonfiction Reading* was written specifically to help you respond to the demands of your state and local standards while meeting the needs of your students.

Purpose of This Book

Each passage in *Differentiated Nonfiction Reading* covers a grade-level appropriate curriculum topic in science, geography, history, or language arts. The Mid-continent Research for Education and Learning (McREL) standard and benchmark related to each passage is listed on pages 9–12.

Each content-area passage is written at three different levels: easy (below grade level), average (at grade level), and challenging (above grade level). After each passage is a set of comprehension questions that all of your students will answer. This enables your students to access the text and concepts at their instructional—rather than frustration—level, while requiring them to meet objective standards, just as they must do on standardized assessments.

Prepare Your Students to Read Content-Area Text

You can prepare your students to read the passages in *Differentiated Nonfiction Reading* by daily reading aloud a short nonfiction selection from another source. Reading content-area text aloud is critical to developing your students' ability to read it themselves.

Discussing content-area concepts with your class is also very important. Remember, however, that discussion can never replace reading aloud since people do not speak using the vocabulary and complex sentence structures of written language.

Readability

All of the passages in *Differentiated Nonfiction Reading* have a reading level calculated by the Flesch-Kincaid Readability Formula. This formula, built into Microsoft Word®, determines a text's readability by calculating the number of words, syllables, and sentences.

Each passage is presented at three levels: easy, average, and challenging. *Easy* is below third-grade level; *average* is at third-grade level; and *challenging* is above third-grade level. The chart on page 13 shows you the specific reading levels of every passage.

To ensure that only you know the reading level at which each student is working, the levels are not printed on the passages. Instead, at the top of the page is a set of books with a specific pattern that will allow you to quickly match students and passages.

Pattern			
Reading Level	**easy** (below grade level)	**average** (at grade level)	**challenging** (above grade level)

Essential Comprehension Skills

Comprehension is the primary goal of any reading task. Students who comprehend expository text not only do better on tests, but they also have more opportunities in life. *Differentiated Nonfiction Reading* will help you to promote the foundation of comprehension skills necessary for a lifetime of learning. The questions following each passage always appear in the same order and cover six vital comprehension skills:

1. **Locating facts**—Questions based on exactly what the text states—*who, what, when, where, why,* and *how many*

2. **Understanding vocabulary in context**—Questions based on the ability to infer word meaning from the syntax and semantics of the surrounding text, as well as the ability to recognize known synonyms and antonyms for a newly encountered word

3. **Determining sequence**—Questions based on chronological order—what happened *first, last,* and *in between*

4. **Identifying conditions**—Questions that ask students to identify similarities and differences or notice cause-and-effect relationships

5. **Making inferences**—Questions that require students to evaluate, make decisions, and draw logical conclusions

6. **Analyzing and visualizing**—Questions that make students draw upon their schema and/or visualization skills to select the correct response (Visualization reinforces the important skill of picturing the text.)

How to Use This Book

You can choose to do whole-class or independent practice. For whole-group practice, you can:

1. Distribute the passages based on students' instructional reading levels.

2. Have students read the text silently and answer the questions either on the comprehension questions page or on one of the Answer Sheets on pages 94–95.

3. Collect all the papers and score them.

4. Return the comprehension questions pages or Answer Sheets to the students, and discuss how they determined their answers.

5. Point out how students had to use their background knowledge to answer certain questions.

You may distribute the passages without revealing the different levels. There are several ways to approach this. If you do not want your students to be aware that the passages are differentiated, organize the passages in small piles by seating arrangement. Then, when you approach a group of desks, you have just the levels you need. An alternative is to make a pile of passages from diamonds to polka dots. Put a finger between the top two levels. Then, as you approach each student, pull the passage from the top (easy), middle (average), or bottom (challenging) layer. You will need to do this quickly and without much hesitation.

Introduction *(cont.)*

How to Use This Book *(cont.)*

You can also announce to your class that all students will read at their own instructional levels. Do not discuss the technicalities of how the reading levels were determined. Just state that every person is reading at his or her own level and then answering the same questions. By making this statement, you can make distributing the three different levels a straightforward process.

If you find that a student is doing well, try giving him or her the next-level-up passage the next time. If he or she displays frustration, be ready to slip the student the lower-level passage.

If you prefer to have the students work independently or in centers, follow this procedure:

1. Create a folder for each student.
2. If needed, make photocopies of the Answer Sheet on page 95 for each class member, and staple the Answer Sheet to the back of each student folder.
3. Each time you want to use a passage, place the appropriate reading level of the passage and the associated comprehension questions in each student's folder.
4. Have students retrieve their folders, read the passage, and answer the questions.
5. Go over the answers with the whole class, or check the folders individually at a convenient time.
6. As an option, you may want to provide a laminated copy of the Answer Key on page 96 in the center, so students can check their own papers.

Teaching Multiple-Choice Response

Whichever method you choose for using the book, it's a good idea to practice as a class how to read a passage and respond to the comprehension questions. In this way, you can demonstrate your own thought processes by "thinking aloud" to figure out an answer. Essentially, this means that you tell your students your thoughts as they come to you.

First, make copies of the practice comprehension questions on page 8, and distribute them to your class. Then, make and display an overhead transparency of the practice reading passage on page 7. Next, read the passage chorally. Studies have found that students of all ages enjoy choral reading, and it is especially helpful for English language learners. Choral reading lets students practice reading fluently in a safe venue because they can read in a whisper or even drop out if they feel the need.

Discuss Question 1: After you've read the passage aloud, ask a student to read the first question aloud. Tell the student NOT to answer the question. Instead, read all the answer choices aloud. Emphasize that reading the choices first is always the best way to approach any multiple-choice question. Since the question is about *locating facts,* reread the first paragraph of the passage aloud as the class follows along. Have the students reread the question silently and make a selection based on the information found. Ask a student who gives the correct response (A) to explain his or her reasoning. Explain that the first question is always the easiest because the answer is stated right in the passage.

Discuss Question 2: The second question is about the *vocabulary* word shown in boldfaced print in the passage. Ask a student to read the question aloud. Teach your students to reread the sentence before, the sentence with, and the sentence after the vocabulary word in the passage. This will give them a context and help them to figure out what the word means. Then, have them substitute the word choices given for the vocabulary term in the passage. For each choice, they should reread the sentence with the substituted word and ask themselves, "Does this make sense?" This will help them to identify the best choice. One by one, substitute the words into the sentence, and read the sentence aloud. It will be obvious which one makes the most sense (C).

Introduction *(cont.)*

Teaching Multiple-Choice Response *(cont.)*

Discuss Question 3: The third question asks about *sequence*. Ask a student to read the question aloud. Write the choices on chart paper or the board. As a class, determine their order of occurrence, and write the numbers one through four next to them. Then, reread the question and make the correct choice (D).

Discuss Question 4: The fourth question is about *cause and effect* or *similarities and differences*. Ask a student to read the question aloud. Teach your students to look for the key words in the question ("after the war") and search for those specific words in the passage. Explain that they may need to look for synonyms for the key words. For this question, ask your students to show where they found the correct response in the passage. Have students explain in their own words how they figured out the correct answer (B). This may be time-consuming at first, but it is an excellent way to help your students learn from each other.

Discuss Question 5: The fifth question asks students to make an *inference*. Ask a student to read the question aloud. Tell your students your thoughts as they occur to you, such as: "Well, the article didn't say the name of the capital city. I've got four choices: Washington, D.C., Lincoln, Boston, and Philadelphia. How can I figure this out if the article didn't tell me? Oh, I know! I'll reread the article one paragraph at a time to see if it gives me any clues. (Reread just the first paragraph.) Wait a minute! Look at the last line in the paragraph. It tells me that the capital is named for him. The article hasn't even mentioned Lincoln yet, and there's no one named Boston or Philadelphia in the article, either. So it's named after George Washington. I'm going to choose (A)."

Discuss Question 6: The sixth question calls for *analysis* or *visualization*. With such questions, some of the answers may be stated in the passage, but others may have different wording. Sometimes one or more of the answers must be visualized to ascertain the correct response.

After having a student read the question aloud, you can say, "This one is tricky. It's telling me to picture a calendar in my mind. This means I need to use what I already know. The answer isn't in the passage. Hmm . . . what makes February different from other months? Let me read the answer choices. (Read choices aloud.) OK. The answer has to be that all of the dates are odd, all of the dates are even, or the month is longer or shorter than all of the other months. Now, let me close my eyes and picture February. No month has only odd or even dates, so that's not right. Is February longer than other months? Because it's winter, it can feel that way! But no, I think what makes February different is that it is short—shorter than any other month. Even when it's a leap year, it only has 29 days! All of the other months have 30 or 31. So the correct answer must be (C)."

Frequent Practice Is Ideal

The passages and comprehension questions in *Differentiated Nonfiction Reading* are time-efficient, allowing your students to practice these skills often. The more your students practice reading and responding to content-area comprehension questions, the more confident and competent they will become. Set aside time to allow your class to do every passage. If you do so, you'll be pleased with your students' improved comprehension of any nonfiction text, both within your classroom and beyond its walls.

Presidents' Day

Over 200 years ago, Americans had to fight a war. They fought to break free from British rule. George Washington led the fight and won. Then, he led America for another eight years. He was the first president. We call him the Father of our Country. Our nation's capital is named after him.

Abraham Lincoln was another president. He did not want people to have **slaves**. He said that one person could not own another. The people in the North said that Lincoln was right. The people in the South said that he was not. This led to the U.S. Civil War. The men from the North fought the men from the South. The troops from the North won the war. When it was over, everyone was free.

Washington and Lincoln had a lot in common. Both believed in freedom. Both had to fight a war to make people free. Both have monuments that honor them. And both of these great leaders were born in February. Now, a day in February honors them. We call it Presidents' Day.

George Washington

Abraham Lincoln

Presidents' Day

Directions: Darken the best answer choice.

1. Who did George Washington fight against?
   - Ⓐ the British
   - Ⓑ Abe Lincoln
   - Ⓒ the Southerners
   - Ⓓ the Northerners

2. What are **slaves**?
   - Ⓐ People who fight.
   - Ⓑ People who do work.
   - Ⓒ People who belong to another person.
   - Ⓓ People who build monuments.

3. What happened first?
   - Ⓐ Abe Lincoln was president.
   - Ⓑ George Washington was president.
   - Ⓒ The northern states and southern states fought each other.
   - Ⓓ The British and the Americans fought a war.

4. After the Civil War,
   - Ⓐ people started to own slaves.
   - Ⓑ all slaves were set free.
   - Ⓒ Americans had to fight the British.
   - Ⓓ the Northerners and Southerners went to war.

5. The capital of the United States of America is
   - Ⓐ Washington, D.C.
   - Ⓑ Lincoln.
   - Ⓒ Boston.
   - Ⓓ Philadelphia.

6. Picture the month of February on the calendar. It has
   - Ⓐ all odd numbers for its dates.
   - Ⓑ all even numbers for its dates.
   - Ⓒ fewer days than any other month.
   - Ⓓ more days than any other month.

Standards Correlation

Each passage and comprehension question in *Differentiated Nonfiction Reading* meets at least one of the following standards and benchmarks, which are used with permission from McREL. Copyright 2010 McREL. Mid-continent Research for Education and Learning, 4601 DTC Boulevard, Suite 500, Denver, CO 80237. Telephone: 303-337-0990. Web site: *www.mcrel.org/standards-benchmarks*. Visit *www.teachercreated.com/standards* for correlations to the Common Core State Standards.

Standards and Benchmarks	Passage Title	Pages
SCIENCE		
Standard 2. Understands Earth's composition and structure **Benchmark 3.** Knows that rock is composed of different combinations of minerals **Benchmark 4.** Knows the composition and properties of soils (e.g., components of soil such as weathered rock, living organisms, products of plants and animals; properties of soil such as color, texture, capacity to retain water, ability to support plant growth)	The Salty Truth	14–17
Standard 4. Understands the principles of heredity and related concepts **Benchmark 1.** Knows that many characteristics of an organism are inherited from its parents (e.g., eye color in human beings, fruit or flower color in plants), and other characteristics result from an individual's interactions with the environment (e.g., people's table manners, ability to ride a bicycle) **Benchmark 2.** Knows that differences exist among individuals of the same kind of plant or animal	The Breeds and Traits of Dogs	18–21
Standard 5. Understands the structure and function of cells and organisms **Benchmark 1.** Knows that plants and animals progress through life cycles of birth, growth and development, reproduction, and death; the details of these life cycles are different for different organisms **Benchmark 2.** Knows that living organisms have distinct structures and body systems that serve specific functions in growth, survival, and reproduction (e.g., various body structures for walking, flying, or swimming) **Benchmark 3.** Knows that the behavior of individual organisms is influenced by internal cues (e.g., hunger) and external cues (e.g., changes in the environment) and that humans and other organisms have senses that help them to detect these cues	Hop Along or Fly High	22–25

Standards Correlation *(cont.)*

Standards and Benchmarks	Passage Title	Pages
SCIENCE *(cont.)*		
Standard 9. Understands the sources and properties of energy **Benchmark 5.** Knows that the pitch of a sound depends on the frequency of the vibrations producing it	Now Hear This!	26–29
Standard 13. Understands the scientific enterprise **Benchmark 1.** Knows that people of all ages, backgrounds, and groups have made contributions to science and technology throughout history	George Eastman Invents the Kodak Moment	30–33
GEOGRAPHY		
Standard 4. Understands the physical and human characteristics of place **Benchmark 1.** Knows how the characteristics of places are shaped by physical and human processes (e.g., effects of agriculture on changing land use and vegetation; effects of settlement on the building of roads; relationship of population distribution to landforms, climate, vegetation, or resources)	Mine Fires That Keep Burning	34–37
Standard 5. Understands the concept of regions **Benchmark 1.** Knows the characteristics of a variety of regions (e.g., landforms, climate, vegetation, shopping, housing, manufacturing, religion, language) **Benchmark 3.** Knows how regions are similar and different in form and function	Cold and Hot Deserts	38–41
Standard 7. Knows the physical processes that shape patterns on Earth's surface **Benchmark 2.** Understands how physical processes help to shape features and patterns on Earth's surface (e.g., the effects of climate and weather on vegetation, erosion and deposition on landforms, mudslides on hills)	Cold and Hot Deserts Mighty Meteors The Life Cycle of a Pond	38–41 42–45 46–49
Standard 8. Understands the characteristics of ecosystems on Earth's surface **Benchmark 1.** Knows the components of ecosystems at a variety of scales (e.g., fungi, insects, plants, and animals in a food chain or food web; fish and marine vegetation in coastal zones; grasses, birds, and insects in grassland areas)	The Life Cycle of a Pond	46–49

Standards and Benchmarks	Passage Title	Pages
GEOGRAPHY (cont.)		
Standard 14. Understands how human actions modify the physical environment **Benchmark 1.** Knows the ways people alter the physical environment (e.g., by creating irrigation projects; clearing the land to make room for houses and shopping centers; planting crops; building roads) **Benchmark 2.** Knows the ways in which the physical environment is stressed by human activities (e.g., changes in climate, air pollution, water pollution, expanding human settlement)	Mine Fires That Keep Burning	34–37
Standard 15. Understands how physical systems affect human systems **Benchmark 4.** Knows natural hazards that occur in the physical environment (e.g., floods, windstorms, tornadoes, earthquakes)	Eerie Earthquakes	50–53
HISTORY		
Standard 2. Understands the history of a local community and how communities in North America varied long ago **Benchmark 2.** Knows geographical settings, economic activities, food, clothing, homes, crafts, and rituals of Native American societies long ago (e.g., Iroquois, Sioux, Hopi, Nez Perce, Inuit, Cherokee)	Pacific Northwest Native Americans	54–57
Standard 3. Understands the people, events, problems, and ideas that were significant in creating the history of their state **Benchmark 1.** Understands differences between the lives of Native Americans or Hawaiians today and their lives 100 years ago **Benchmark 3.** Understands the interactions that occurred between the Native Americans or Hawaiians and the first European, African, and Asian-Pacific explorers and settlers in the state or region	Pacific Northwest Native Americans	54–57
Benchmark 9. Understands the influence of geography on the history of the state or region, and issues and approaches to problems (e.g., land use, environmental problems)	Mine Fires That Keep Burning	34–37
Standard 4. Understands how democratic values came to be, and how they have been exemplified by people, events, and symbols **Benchmark 1.** Understands the basic ideas set forth in the Declaration of Independence and the U.S. Constitution and the figures responsible for these documents	The U.S. Constitution	58–61

Standards Correlation (cont.)

Standards and Benchmarks	Passage Title	Pages
HISTORY (cont.)		
Standard 4 (cont.) **Benchmark 4.** Understands the accomplishments of ordinary people in historical situations and how each struggled for individual rights or for the common good	Oral Lee Brown Opens the Door	66–69
Benchmark 6. Understands historical figures who believed in the fundamental democratic values (e.g., justice, truth, equality, the rights of the individual, responsibility for the common good, voting rights) and the significance of these people both in their historical context and today **Benchmark 7.** Understands how historical figures in the U.S. and in other parts of the world have advanced the rights of individuals and promoted the common good and the character traits that made them successful (e.g., persistence, problem solving, moral responsibility, respect for others)	Condoleezza Rice, Former U.S. Secretary of State	70–73
Benchmark 9. Knows the history of events and the historic figures responsible for such historical documents as the Mayflower Compact, the Declaration of Independence, the U.S. Constitution, the Bill of Rights, and the Emancipation Proclamation	The U.S. Constitution The Bill of Rights	58–61 62–65
LANGUAGE ARTS*		
Standard 7. Uses reading skills and strategies to understand and interpret a variety of informational texts **Benchmark 1.** Uses reading skills and strategies to understand a variety of informational texts (e.g., textbooks, biographical sketches, letters, diaries, directions, procedures, magazines)	Guinea Pigs (Journal Entries)	74–77
Benchmark 2. Knows the defining characteristics of a variety of informational texts (e.g., textbooks, biographical sketches, letters, diaries, directions, procedures, magazines)	Dr. Seuss Loved Green Eggs and Ham (Biography)	78–81
Benchmark 3. Uses text organizers (e.g., headings, topic and summary sentences, graphic features, typeface, chapter titles) to determine the main ideas and to locate information in a text	Delicious Discoveries (Magazine Article)	82–85
Benchmark 5. Summarizes and paraphrases information in texts (e.g., includes the main idea and significant supporting details of a reading selection)	Beyond Belief (Web Site)	86–89
Benchmark 6. Uses prior knowledge and experience to understand and respond to new information **Benchmark 7.** Understands structural patterns or organization in informational texts (e.g., chronological, logical, or sequential order; compare-and-contrast; cause-and-effect; proposition and support)	The Miracle on the Hudson (Newspaper Article)	90–93

* Each passage in this book meets the language arts standard of some or all of these benchmarks. The language arts passages are listed here because they were designed to specifically address these benchmarks.

Reading Levels Chart

Content Area and Title	Easy ◇	Average ☆	Challenging ◯
SCIENCE			
The Salty Truth	2.3	3.4	4.7
The Breeds and Traits of Dogs	2.0	3.0	4.0
Hop Along or Fly High	2.0	3.1	4.2
Now Hear This!*	2.8	3.5	4.7
George Eastman Invents the Kodak Moment	2.8	3.8	4.9
GEOGRAPHY			
Mine Fires That Keep Burning	2.7	3.6	4.5
Cold and Hot Deserts	2.7	3.5	4.5
Mighty Meteors	2.8	3.6	4.3
The Life Cycle of a Pond	2.5	3.4	4.6
Eerie Earthquakes	2.8	3.8	4.8
HISTORY			
Pacific Northwest Native Americans	2.9	3.7	4.8
The U.S. Constitution*	2.7	3.5	4.8
The Bill of Rights*	2.5	3.5	4.9
Oral Lee Brown Opens the Door	2.3	3.3	4.4
Condoleezza Rice, Former U.S. Secretary of State	2.9	3.9	4.7
LANGUAGE ARTS			
Guinea Pigs (Journal Entries)	2.1	3.2	4.0
Dr. Seuss Loved Green Eggs and Ham (Biography)	2.2	3.0	4.0
Delicious Discoveries (Magazine Article)	2.5	3.4	4.4
Beyond Belief (Web Site)	2.5	3.5	4.5
The Miracle on the Hudson (Newspaper Article)	2.7	3.6	4.8

*These passages may have higher reading levels than what is indicated here because of repetitive multisyllabic words such as frequency, government, and Constitution.

The Salty Truth

A mineral is a substance that occurs in nature. It has a crystal structure. It is inorganic. This means that it is not alive. It never was. Salt is a common mineral. It has 14,000 known uses. It can keep food from going bad. It is used to make ice cream, cheese, and paper. It dissolves, or melts, in water. When the water dries up, it reappears as tiny crystals. You may have some on your kitchen table.

People built the first roads to trade salt. In Africa, whole kingdoms were based on this trade. The Africans had gold. They wanted salt. So they traded gold for salt. Salt traders paid to use their roads, too. Long ago, a pound of gold bought a pound of salt! The ancient Romans even paid their workers with salt. They called the wages *salarium*. It is the basis for our word *salary*.

Why is salt so valuable? Our bodies cannot make it. Yet we need it. Salt helps to keep the fluid in our blood cells. It is used by our nerves and muscles. It helps us to get nutrients from food. And people found that by rubbing salt into meat, it would stay **edible** for a long time.

Ice and snow are frozen water. Mixing salt with ice or snow makes both melt. And if salt is mixed with water and kept at a cold temperature, the water does not harden into ice. Instead, it forms slush. In places with ice and snow, large trucks spread salt on the streets. This helps to keep the roads passable. But some places spread sand instead. Why? Salt causes rust on the steel parts of bridges. It breaks up the road pavement, too. It also gets into the soil. Salt can kill trees and bushes planted close to the street. And when the snow and ice melt, the salt dissolves in the water. Then it flows into streams and rivers. This adds salt to the fresh water. It is not good for the things living there.

Salt may be dug from underground mines. It may be dug from aboveground salt mountains. It must always be refined. This separates the salt from other minerals.

You can get too much of a good thing. Eating too much salt will raise your blood pressure. Seawater has salt in it. You cannot drink it. Drinking too much seawater will kill you. In the nations of Israel and Jordan, the people do not have enough water. So they take salt water from the Dead Sea. They boil it. It turns into steam. When the steam condenses back into water, it is fresh. Then people can drink it.

The Salty Truth

A mineral is a substance that occurs in nature and has a crystalline structure. It is inorganic, which means it is not alive and never was. Salt is a common mineral. It has 14,000 known uses. Some of these include keeping food from rotting and making ice cream, cheese, and paper. Salt dissolves in water. Yet when the water dries up, it reappears as crystals. You may have some on your kitchen table.

Salt is necessary for life. People built the first roads so they could trade with it. In Africa, entire kingdoms were based on the salt trade. The Africans had a lot of gold and needed salt. So they traded gold for salt. They charged the salt traders to use their roads, too. Long ago, a pound of salt was worth a pound of gold! The ancient Romans even paid their workers with salt. They called the wages *salarium*. It is the basis for our word *salary*.

What makes salt so valuable? Our bodies cannot make it, yet we need it. Salt helps to maintain the fluid in our blood cells. Our nerves and muscles use it. It also helps our intestines to get nutrients from food. Meat rots when exposed to rain and heat. But people discovered that by rubbing salt into meat, it would remain **edible** for a long time.

Ice and snow are frozen water. Ice and snow melt when mixed with salt. And if salt is mixed with water and kept at a cold temperature, the salt stops the water from freezing into hard ice. Instead, it forms slush. In places with ice and snow during the winter, large trucks spread salt on the roads. This keeps the roads passable. But now some places spread sand. Why? Salt causes rust on the steel parts of bridges. It damages the road pavement and gets into the soil. Salt can kill trees and bushes planted close to the street. When the snow and ice melt, the salt dissolves in the water and flows into streams and rivers. It adds salt to the fresh water. It is bad for the things living there.

Salt may be dug from underground mines or aboveground salt mountains. No matter where it comes from, it must be refined to separate the salt from other minerals.

You can get too much of a good thing. Eating too much salt will raise your blood pressure. You cannot drink seawater because it is salty. Drinking too much will kill you. In the nations of Israel and Jordan, the people need drinking water. So they take salt water from the Dead Sea. They heat it until it turns into steam. When the steam condenses, it is fresh water. Then it is safe to drink.

The Salty Truth

A mineral is a substance that occurs in nature and has a crystalline structure. It is inorganic, which means it has never been alive. Salt is a common mineral with 14,000 known uses. Some of these include preserving food and making ice cream, cheese, and paper products. Salt dissolves in water, but when the water evaporates, it reappears as crystals.

Salt is necessary for life. People built the first roads to transport it. In Africa, entire kingdoms were based on the salt trade. The Africans had a lot of gold and wanted salt. So they traded gold for salt. Long ago, a pound of salt was worth a pound of gold! They also charged the salt traders to use their roads. The ancient Romans even paid their workers with salt. They called the wages *salarium*, which is the basis for our word *salary*.

Salt is valuable because our bodies need it and cannot make it. Salt helps to maintain the fluid in our blood cells. Our nerves and muscles use it. It also helps our intestines to absorb nutrients from food. Meat rots when exposed to heat or dampness. But people discovered that by rubbing salt into meat, it would remain **edible** for a long time.

Ice and snow are both forms of frozen water. If you mix salt with either one, it melts. And if salt is mixed with water and kept at a cold temperature, the salt prevents the water from turning into hard ice. It forms slush. In places with ice and snow during the winter, large trucks spread salt on the roads to keep them passable. But some places now spread sand instead because salt causes rust on the steel parts of bridges. It damages the road pavement and gets into the soil, killing trees and bushes planted close to the street. Also, when the snow and ice melt, the salt will dissolve in the water and flow into streams and rivers. This adds salt to fresh water and is bad for the things living there.

Salt may be dug from underground mines or aboveground salt mountains. No matter where it comes from, it must be refined to separate the salt from other minerals.

You can get too much of a good thing. Eating too much salt will raise your blood pressure. You cannot drink seawater because it has salt in it. In fact, drinking too much seawater will kill you. In the nations of Israel and Jordan, the people need drinking water. They take salt water from the Dead Sea and boil it until it turns into steam. When the steam condenses, it is fresh water. Then it is safe to drink.

The Salty Truth

Directions: Darken the best answer choice.

1. Salt is a
   - Ⓐ man-made substance.
   - Ⓑ mineral.
   - Ⓒ salarium.
   - Ⓓ salary.

2. The word **edible** means
   - Ⓐ able to be eaten.
   - Ⓑ changed color.
   - Ⓒ kept warm.
   - Ⓓ kept cold.

3. What happens first?
   - Ⓐ Salt gets into the soil.
   - Ⓑ Trucks spread salt on the icy roads.
   - Ⓒ A pine tree planted along the road dies.
   - Ⓓ Snow falls.

4. Which statement is true?
   - Ⓐ We need salt and cannot get too much of it.
   - Ⓑ We don't need salt and shouldn't eat any.
   - Ⓒ We need salt, but too much is bad for us.
   - Ⓓ The only way to get salt is to mine it from underground.

5. When seawater is boiled, the vapor
   - Ⓐ is salty.
   - Ⓑ is fresh water.
   - Ⓒ cannot be collected.
   - Ⓓ needs salt added to it so people can use it.

6. When salt gets onto steel, it causes the metal to
   - Ⓐ turn into a liquid.
   - Ⓑ become stronger.
   - Ⓒ change into a vapor.
   - Ⓓ rust.

The Breeds and Traits of Dogs

Do you have a dog? Even if you do not own a dog, you have seen different dogs. Some are big, and others are small. Some have short hair; some have long hair. Dogs come in all shapes, sizes, and colors. Why?

People breed dogs to do certain jobs. Some dogs, like retrievers, pick up dead animals. When a hunter shoots a bird, his dog brings it back. Some dogs herd sheep or cows. Why? Sheep may wander off. A dog makes them stay with the group. St. Bernard dogs were first bred where there is deep snow. These big dogs can find people under snowbanks. They dig them out and save their lives. Some dogs are bred just to sit on a person's lap and keep him or her company. Long ago, kings and queens liked to hold dogs, so many royal courts had some kind of small dog.

To breed dogs, people find the traits they like in a male and a female. The traits can be things like size, color, personality, or the **ability** to run fast. People breed these dogs together. Then their puppies have the good traits from both parents.

Puppies always look like one or both of their parents. Two poodles will have poodle puppies. They will not have beagles! Some people like cockapoos. One dog parent is a cocker spaniel. The other is a poodle. The puppies will not look just like a cocker spaniel. They will not look just like a poodle, either. They will have traits from each parent. Some may have curly poodle hair. Others may have long, wavy cocker spaniel hair. Or a pup's coat may be a mix of the two hair types.

Poodles do not shed their hair. Cocker spaniels do. That means that cockapoo pups may shed. Or they may not. Each puppy will have the shedding trait of one parent or the other.

Even though dogs don't all look alike, they share many behaviors. They bark and eat meat. They like to smell things. They wag their tails when they are glad. They growl or whine when they are upset. They like to be members of a pack and view their human families as their packs.

The Breeds and Traits of Dogs

Do you have a dog? Even if you do not own a dog, you have seen different dogs. Some are big, and some are small. Some have short hair, and others have long hair. Dogs come in all shapes, sizes, and colors. Why?

People breed dogs to do certain jobs. Some dogs, like Labrador retrievers, pick up dead animals. When a hunter shoots a bird, the dog brings it back. Other dogs are bred to herd sheep or cows. Sheep may wander away if a dog does not make them stay with the group. St. Bernard dogs were first bred where there is deep snow. These big dogs can find people buried under snowbanks. They can dig them out and save their lives. Some dogs are bred just to sit on a person's lap and be good company. Long ago, kings and queens liked to hold dogs. Many royal courts had some kind of small dog.

To breed dogs, people look for traits they like in a male and a female. The traits can be things like size, color, personality, or the **ability** to run fast. People breed these dogs together. Then the puppies have the good traits from both parents.

Puppies always look like one or both of their parents. Two poodles will produce poodle puppies. They will not have beagles! Some people like cockapoos. One dog parent is a cocker spaniel, and the other parent is a poodle. The puppies will not look just like a cocker spaniel. They will not look just like a poodle, either. They will have traits from each parent. Some may have curly poodle hair, and others may have long, wavy cocker spaniel hair. A pup's coat may also be a mix of the two hair types.

Poodles do not shed their hair, but cocker spaniels do. That means that cockapoo pups may shed, or they may not. Each puppy is an individual and will have the shedding trait of one parent or the other.

Even though dogs don't all look alike, they do have traits in common, especially behaviors. They bark and eat meat. They like to smell things. They wag their tails when they are happy and growl or whine when they get upset. They like to be members of a pack and view their human families as their packs.

The Breeds and Traits of Dogs

Do you have a dog? Even if you do not own a dog, you have seen many different dogs. You know that some are big and others are little. Some have short hair, while others have long hair. Dogs come in all shapes, sizes, and colors. Have you ever wondered why?

People breed dogs to do certain jobs. Some dogs, like Labrador retrievers, pick up dead animals and carry them to a person. A hunter shoots a bird, and his dog brings it back. Other dogs herd sheep or cows. (Sheep often wander away if a dog does not keep them with the group.) St. Bernards were originally bred where there is deep snow. These big dogs can find people under snowbanks, dig them out, and save their lives. Some dogs are bred to be companions and sit on laps. Long ago, kings and queens liked to hold dogs, so many royal courts had some kind of small dog.

To breed dogs, people look for excellent traits in a male and a female. The traits can be things like size, coat color, personality, or the **ability** to run rapidly. People breed these dogs together, hoping that the puppies will have the good traits from both parents.

Puppies will always look like one or both of their parents. Two poodles will produce poodle puppies. They will never have beagles! Some people like mixed breeds such as cockapoos. One dog parent is a cocker spaniel, and the other is a poodle. The puppies will not look just like a cocker spaniel nor will they look just like a poodle. They will have traits from each parent. Some may have curly poodle hair, and others may have long, wavy cocker spaniel hair. A puppy's coat may also be a mix of these hair types.

Poodles do not shed their hair, but cocker spaniels do. That means that some cockapoo pups shed, while others may not. Each puppy is an individual and will have the shedding trait of one parent or the other.

Even though dogs don't all look alike, they do share common behaviors. They bark, eat meat, and like to smell things. They wag their tails when they are happy and growl or whine when they are upset. They like to be members of a pack and view their human families as their packs.

The Breeds and Traits of Dogs

Directions: Darken the best answer choice.

1. When people breed dogs, they want the puppies to
   - Ⓐ have the parents' best traits.
   - Ⓑ be a different color than the parents.
   - Ⓒ bark more than the parents do.
   - Ⓓ be much larger than the parents are.

2. The word **ability** means
   - Ⓐ agrees to.
   - Ⓑ able to.
   - Ⓒ unable to.
   - Ⓓ refuses to.

3. What happens first?
   - Ⓐ A retriever uses its nose to find a duck.
   - Ⓑ A hunter and his retriever share a meal of roasted duck.
   - Ⓒ A hunter shoots a duck.
   - Ⓓ A retriever brings the duck to the hunter.

4. A St. Bernard dog was bred to
   - Ⓐ pick up dead animals.
   - Ⓑ herd sheep.
   - Ⓒ sit on a person's lap.
   - Ⓓ rescue people.

5. Every dog
   - Ⓐ gets some traits from each of its parents.
   - Ⓑ sheds its fur.
   - Ⓒ likes to eat vegetables.
   - Ⓓ wags its tail when it is afraid.

6. Lap dogs were first bred for
   - Ⓐ protection.
   - Ⓑ royal families.
   - Ⓒ hunters.
   - Ⓓ farmers.

Hop Along or Fly High

Do you like birds? It can be fun to hear them sing and watch them fly. But not all birds can fly. It takes more energy to fly than to hop or walk. So if a bird lives where it does not have **predators** on the ground, over time, it will stop flying. For example, penguins do not have land predators. And they cannot fly. New Zealand is an island. It has few predators. As a result, several kinds of birds that cannot fly live there.

Most birds that live in trees hop. It is the best way to get from branch to branch. The birds that hop in trees also hop on the ground. Why? Hopping covers more distance with less energy than walking. The birds that are the best fliers are nearly helpless on their legs. This includes hummingbirds, swallows, and swifts.

Birds migrate if they live where it gets cold in the winter. This means they fly south. As the days grow shorter in the fall, these birds shed their feathers. Their bodies react to the length of daylight. Losing feathers is called *molting*, and it takes energy. That is why birds are so much quieter in August and September than in the spring. They are using their energy to molt instead of sing. With fewer feathers, the birds are less heavy. That helps them on the long flight south.

But why do birds migrate at all? It takes a lot of effort to fly hundreds of miles south. Then, in the spring, they fly back again. Why not just live where it's always warm? The answer is food. The North has more food in the spring and summer. Many insects lay eggs in the fall. They hatch the next spring. This means that the birds that eat insects have no food in the winter. They must go south.

In the spring, the bugs in the North hatch. Bird babies hatch about the same time. Baby birds need a lot of food. Bugs are full of protein. A high-protein diet helps the babies to grow their first feathers. Even the birds that do not eat insects themselves will feed them to their young.

What about the birds that live in the South year-round? They can share their food supply in the winter. But if the migrating birds didn't leave in the spring, fewer baby birds would survive. The amount of food in the South stays the same all the time. So when lots of baby birds hatched, there would be too many birds and too little food. Some would starve. In the spring, the bugs in the North create a feast for birds. That's why songbirds that live in the North lay many more eggs than those that live in the South.

Hop Along or Fly High

Do you like birds? You may enjoy listening to them sing and watching them fly. But not all birds can fly. It takes more energy to fly than to hop or walk. So if a bird lives in a place that does not have **predators** on the ground, over time, it will stop flying. Instead, it will hop or walk. For example, penguins do not have land predators, and they cannot fly. New Zealand is an island with few predators. That's why several kinds of birds that cannot fly live there.

Most birds that live in trees hop. It is the easiest way to move from branch to branch. The birds that hop in trees also hop on the ground. Hopping covers more distance with less energy than walking. The birds that are the best fliers are nearly helpless on their legs. This includes hummingbirds, swallows, and swifts.

Birds that live where it gets cold in the winter migrate. This means they fly south. As the days grow shorter in the fall, these birds shed their feathers. Their bodies react to the length of daylight. Losing feathers is called *molting,* and it takes energy. That is why birds are so much quieter in August and September than in the spring. With fewer feathers, the birds are lighter in weight, which helps them on the long flight south.

But why do birds migrate at all? It is a huge effort to fly hundreds of miles south, and then, in the spring, to fly back again. Why don't they just stay where it's warm year-round? The answer is food. In the spring and summer months, the North has more food. Many insects lay eggs in the fall that hatch the next spring. This means that birds that eat insects have no food supply in the winter, so they must go south.

In the spring, the bugs in the North hatch. Birds have their babies in the spring. Baby birds demand food all the time. Bugs are full of protein, and a high-protein diet helps the baby birds to grow their first feathers. Even those birds that do not eat insects themselves will feed them to their young.

What about the birds that live in the South year-round? They can share their food supply in the winter, but if the migrating birds didn't leave in the spring, fewer baby birds would survive. The amount of food in the South stays the same all the time. So when baby birds hatched, there would be too many birds and too little food, and some would starve. The bugs in the North create a feast for birds each spring. That's why songbirds that live in the North lay so many more eggs than those that live in the South.

Hop Along or Fly High

Do you like birds? Many people enjoy listening to birds sing and watching them fly—although not all birds do fly. It takes more energy to fly than to hop or walk. This means that if a bird lives in a place without ground **predators**, over time, it will stop flying and will hop or walk instead. For example, penguins do not have land predators, and they cannot fly. New Zealand is an island with few predators, which is why several kinds of birds that cannot fly live there.

Most birds that live in trees hop since it is the easiest way to move from branch to branch. The birds that hop in trees also hop on the ground. Hopping covers more distance with less energy than walking. Hummingbirds, swallows, and swifts are some of the best fliers. Yet being such good fliers means that they are nearly helpless on their legs.

Birds that live where it gets cold in the winter migrate by flying south. As the days grow shorter in the fall, these birds shed their feathers. Their bodies react to the length of daylight. Losing feathers is called *molting*, and it takes energy, which is why birds are so much quieter in August and September than in the spring. With fewer feathers, the birds are lighter in weight, which helps them on their long flight south.

But why do birds migrate at all? It is an enormous effort to fly hundreds of miles south, and then, in the spring, to fly back again. Why don't they just stay where it's warm year-round? The answer is food. In the spring and summer months, the North has more food. Many insects lay eggs in the fall that hatch the next spring. This means that birds that eat insects have no food supply in the winter, so they must go south.

In the spring, the bugs in the North hatch about the same time that baby birds hatch. Baby birds demand food all the time. Bugs are full of protein, and a high-protein diet helps the baby birds to grow their first feathers. Therefore, even birds that do not eat insects themselves will feed them to their young.

What about the birds that live in the South year-round? They can share their food supply in the winter, but if the migrating birds didn't leave in the spring, fewer baby birds would survive. The amount of food in the South stays the same all the time. Therefore, when baby birds hatched, there would be too many birds and too little food, and some would starve. The bugs in the North offer a feast for birds each spring. That's why the songbirds that live in the North lay so many more eggs than those that live in the South.

Hop Along or Fly High

Directions: Darken the best answer choice.

1. Eating bugs helps baby birds to
   - (A) grow feathers.
   - (B) learn to sing.
   - (C) learn to fly.
   - (D) hide from predators.

2. The word **predators** means animals that
   - (A) migrate.
   - (B) do not migrate.
   - (C) are eaten by other animals.
   - (D) eat other animals.

3. It is early March in the South. What will happen this month?
   - (A) The Northern birds will fly north.
   - (B) The Southern birds will fly north.
   - (C) The Northern birds will fly south.
   - (D) The Southern birds will lay their eggs in the North and then fly home.

4. Birds molt in order to
   - (A) find a mate.
   - (B) find bugs to feed their babies.
   - (C) weigh less before a long flight.
   - (D) build a nest.

5. Northern birds that eat seeds and berries migrate. Why?
   - (A) They need to eat bugs during the winter.
   - (B) They cannot find enough food because it may be beneath snow and ice.
   - (C) They cannot find a mate if they don't migrate.
   - (D) They don't know how to build nests.

6. What does each species of bird do best?
   - (A) walk
   - (B) hop
   - (C) fly
   - (D) It depends upon the kind of bird.

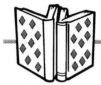

Now Hear This!

Sound is waves. You cannot see them. But they make the air move. They **vibrate**. The waves race through the air. They go 1,125 feet per second. Without air, there are no sound waves. You may have heard a person ask, "If a tree falls in the woods and no one is there to hear it, does it make a sound?" The answer is yes! There is air, so sound waves happen. It doesn't matter if the noise is heard. Outer space has no air. There are no sounds in space.

Electricity can make sound. That is why we get sounds from radios, TVs, and speakers. First, electric current flows to an amplifier. This sends energy to the speaker. The speaker has an electromagnet inside. The electric charge makes the electromagnet move. It vibrates. It makes sound waves.

Phones use electricity. They get and send sounds. First, you speak. The sound waves move the diaphragm in your phone. This makes an electric current. It may go through wires. It may go to a cell tower. Then it reaches the other person's phone. Once there, the current energizes a magnet. The magnet moves. It is inside the phone's diaphragm. This recreates the sound waves. The person hears your voice.

A sound's frequency tells how fast the sound waves vibrate. The frequency determines the sound's pitch. *Frequency* is the number of vibrations, or wave peaks, arriving each second. Long waves have more distance from one peak to the next. These have a low frequency and a low pitch. Short waves have less distance from one peak to the next. These waves have a high frequency. All sound waves move through the air at the same speed. But with a high frequency, more waves reach your ear each second. With a low frequency, fewer waves reach your ear each second.

Humans can only hear some sounds. We do not hear the high frequencies that dogs do. That is how underground "invisible fences" work. The dog wears a radio collar. The wire under the ground transmits a high-frequency sound. If the dog tries to leave the yard, it hears the noise. The noise warns it to stop. If it keeps going, it will be shocked. The dog hates it! The dog learns to stay in the yard.

Humans do not hear very low frequencies, either. Giraffes make low-frequency sounds. Some people, even those who work in zoos, think that giraffes are silent. They never hear them make noise. But that is just because we do not hear their sounds. Why do they make low-frequency sounds? In the wild, giraffes live in herds. They roam the grassy plains in Africa. If a giraffe gets lost, it calls out to its herd. Its low-frequency sound will go farther than a high-frequency one. And the lions that want to eat it cannot hear its call. Whales, elephants, and rhinos use low-frequency calls, too.

Now Hear This!

Sound is waves. You cannot see them, but they make the air move. They **vibrate**. These waves race through the air at 1,125 feet per second. Without air, there are no sound waves. You may have heard someone ask, "If a tree falls in the woods and no one is there to hear it, does it make a sound?" The answer is yes! There is air, so sound waves happen. It doesn't matter if anyone hears it or not. There is no air in outer space. This means that there are no sounds in space.

Electricity can make sounds. This is how we get sounds from loudspeakers, radios, and TVs. Electric current flows to an amplifier. This sends energy to the speaker. The speaker has an electromagnet inside. The electricity makes the electromagnet vibrate. It creates the sound waves.

Phones use electricity to send and get sounds, too. First, you speak into the mouthpiece. The sound waves move the diaphragm in the phone. This makes an electric current. It may travel through wires. It may go to a cell tower. Then it reaches the other person's phone. Once there, the current energizes a magnet. The magnet moves inside the receiver's diaphragm. This recreates the sound waves. The person hears your voice.

A sound's frequency tells how fast the sound waves vibrate. The frequency determines the sound's pitch. *Frequency* is the number of vibrations, or wave peaks, arriving each second. Long waves have more distance from one peak to the next. These have a low frequency and a low pitch. Short waves have less distance from one peak to the next. These waves have a high frequency. All sound waves move through the air at the same speed. But with a high frequency, more waves reach your ear each second. With a low frequency, fewer waves reach your ear each second.

Humans can only hear certain frequencies. We cannot hear some high-frequency noises. Dogs and wolves can hear them. That's how underground "invisible fences" keep dogs inside a yard. The dog wears a radio collar. If the dog tries to leave the yard, the wire under the ground transmits a high-frequency sound. The sound warns the dog to stop. If it continues to leave, it will be shocked. The dog hates this, but the shock trains it to stay in the yard.

We humans cannot hear the other end of the sound spectrum, either. Giraffes make low-frequency sounds. Some people, even those who work in zoos, think that giraffes are silent. They never hear them make any noise. But that's just because we can't hear their sounds. Why do they use low-frequency sounds? In the wild, giraffes live in herds. They roam grassy plains in Africa. If a giraffe gets lost, it will call to its herd. Its low-frequency sound will travel farther than a high-frequency one. Even better, the lions that want to eat the lone giraffe cannot hear its call. Whales, elephants, and rhinoceroses use low-frequency calls, too.

Now Hear This!

Sound is invisible waves that make air move. The air **vibrates** as sound waves race through it at 1,125 feet per second. Without air, there are no sound waves. You may have heard someone ask, "If a tree falls in the woods and no one is there to hear it, does it make a sound?" The answer is yes! Since there is air in the woods, sound waves occur. It doesn't matter if they are heard or not. There is no air in outer space, which means there are no sounds there.

Electricity can generate sound. This is how we get sounds from loudspeakers, radios, and TVs. Electric current flows to an amplifier. This sends energy to the speaker. The speaker has an electromagnet inside. The electricity makes the electromagnet vibrate. It creates the sound waves.

Phones use electricity to send and receive sounds, too. First, you speak into the mouthpiece. The sound waves move the diaphragm in the phone. This creates an electric current that may travel through wires or to a cell tower. When it reaches the other person's phone, a current energizes a magnet. It moves inside the receiver's diaphragm. This recreates the sound waves of your voice.

A sound's frequency tells how fast the sound waves vibrate. The frequency determines the sound's pitch. *Frequency* is the number of vibrations, or wave peaks, arriving each second. Long waves have more distance from one peak to the next. These have a low frequency and a low pitch. Short waves have less distance from one peak to the next. These waves have a high frequency. All sound waves move through the air at the same speed. But with a high frequency, more waves reach your ear each second. With a low frequency, fewer waves reach your ear each second.

Humans can only hear certain frequencies. We cannot hear the high-frequency noises that dogs can. That's how underground "invisible fences" keep dogs inside. The dog wears a radio collar. If the dog tries to leave the yard, the wire under the ground transmits a high-frequency sound. The sound warns the dog to stop. If it continues to leave, it will be shocked. The dog hates this, but the shock trains it to stay inside the borders.

We humans cannot hear the other end of the sound spectrum, either. Giraffes make low-frequency sounds. Some people, even those who work in zoos, think that giraffes are silent because they never hear them make noise. But that's just because people can't hear the sounds they make. Why do they make low-frequency sounds? Wild giraffes live in herds. They roam the grassy plains in Africa. If a giraffe gets separated from the others, it will call to them. Its low-frequency sound will travel farther than a high-frequency one. Even better, the lions that want to eat the lone giraffe cannot hear its call. Whales, elephants, and rhinoceroses use low-frequency calls, too.

Now Hear This!

Directions: Darken the best answer choice.

1. The part inside a cell phone that creates the sound waves is the
   Ⓐ battery.
   Ⓑ wires.
   Ⓒ diaphragm.
   Ⓓ screen.

2. The word **vibrates** means
   Ⓐ moves.
   Ⓑ hums.
   Ⓒ heats up.
   Ⓓ cools off.

3. What happens third?
   Ⓐ Electricity goes to an amplifier inside a speaker.
   Ⓑ You hear your favorite song.
   Ⓒ An electromagnet vibrates.
   Ⓓ Sound waves move through the air.

4. Which animal does not make a low-frequency sound?
   Ⓐ a whale
   Ⓑ a giraffe
   Ⓒ a lion
   Ⓓ a rhinoceros

5. Outer space is silent because there is
   Ⓐ nobody to hear the sound.
   Ⓑ no air.
   Ⓒ no gravity.
   Ⓓ no water.

6. Most dogs can hear
   Ⓐ higher frequencies than humans can.
   Ⓑ lower frequencies than humans can.
   Ⓒ none of the same frequencies that humans can.
   Ⓓ fewer sounds than humans.

George Eastman Invents the Kodak Moment

Do you like photographs? Then thank George Eastman. He was born in 1854. He had two sisters. His dad ran a school. When George was eight years old, his dad died. His mom could not run the school. She had to take in boarders. The boarders paid to live with the family. When George was fourteen, he quit school. He got a job. He had to help pay the bills.

Later, George worked at a bank. But he wanted to take photos. Back then, taking a photo was hard to do. Cameras were big. They weighed a lot. They were as big as microwave ovens! No one could hold one still and take a picture. Cameras were set up on three legs. Cameras used glass plates. Wet chemicals were used, too.

George knew there had to be a better way. He worked with dry chemicals. Then he made a machine. It put chemicals onto dry plates. This made photography less messy. In 1880, he started a business. But it was still hard to take photos. Then, in 1885, George invented film on a roll. This was a big step forward. It made taking pictures easy. People loved film. Yet few took photos. Almost no one had a camera.

Brownie Camera

George wanted everyone to take pictures. He wanted the camera to be as "common as a pencil." In 1900, he made the Brownie camera. It was small. It was light. A child could hold it. It did not cost much. Lots of people could buy one. People were glad. They wanted to take photos. George's company could hardly keep up with the demand for Brownie cameras.

George made up his company's name. He liked the letter "k." He called it Kodak. George was kind to his workers. He shared with them the money his business made. He bought life insurance for them. This means that if a worker died, his or her family would get some money. If a worker got hurt, George made sure he or she saw a doctor. When a worker grew old, George gave him or her a small sum of money. It came each month until the person died. Kodak workers were the first in the United States to have such **benefits**.

By 1902, George was rich. He started free dental clinics for kids. He gave money to schools with African American students. He wanted to help African Americans go to college. He said that educated workers were the best kind. He gave money to start a hospital, too. When George died in 1932, he left all he had to a college.

Now, even cell phones can take photos. It all started with George. He knew that we all want to take photos.

George Eastman Invents the Kodak Moment

Do you like to take photographs? Then you can thank George Eastman. He was born in 1854. He had two sisters. His dad ran a school. When George was eight years old, his dad died. His mom could not run the school. She had to take in boarders. They paid to live with the family. When George was fourteen, he dropped out of school. He took a job. His pay helped to keep his family going.

Later, George worked at a bank. But what he really liked were photographs. At that time, taking a photo was hard to do. Cameras were big and heavy. They were the size of microwave ovens! No one could hold one still long enough to take a picture. The camera was set on three legs called a tripod. Cameras used glass plates. Wet chemicals were used to make the picture, too.

George knew there had to be a better way. He started to work with dry chemicals. He invented a machine. It put chemicals onto dry plates. This made photography less messy. He started his own business in 1880. But it was still hard to take a good picture. Then, in 1885, George invented film on a roll. This made taking a picture easier. Photographers loved film. Yet only a few people owned cameras.

Brownie Camera

George wanted everyone to take pictures. He said the camera should be as "common as a pencil." In 1900, he invented the Brownie camera. It was small. Even a child could hold it! Best of all, it did not cost much. Lots of people could own one. People wanted to take photos. George's company could hardly keep up with the demand for these cameras.

George loved the letter "k" and made up the company's name: Kodak. He was kind to his workers. He shared with them the profits from his business. He bought life insurance for them. That way if a worker died, his or her family would get some money. If a worker got hurt, George made sure he or she saw a doctor. When a person got too old to work, George gave him or her a little bit of money each month until the person died. Kodak workers were the first in the United States to have such **benefits**.

By 1902, George was rich. He started free dental clinics for children. He also gave money to schools with African American students. He wanted to help African Americans go to college. He said that educated workers were the best kind. He donated money to start a hospital, too. When George died in 1932, he left his fortune to a college.

Today, even cell phones can take photos. It all started with George. He knew that we all want to take photos.

George Eastman Invents the Kodak Moment

Do you enjoy taking photographs? You can thank George Eastman. He was born in 1854 and had two sisters. His dad ran a school. When George was just eight years old, his dad died. His mom could not run the school, so she took in boarders. These people paid to live with the family. When George was fourteen, he dropped out of school and took a job to help pay his family's bills.

Later, George worked at a bank. But what he really liked were photographs. At that time, taking a photo was difficult. Cameras were the size of microwave ovens! Nobody could hold one still long enough to take a picture. So the camera was set up on three legs called a tripod. Cameras used glass plates and wet chemicals.

George knew there had to be a better way. So he invented a machine that put chemicals onto dry plates. This made photography less messy. He started his own business in 1880. But it was still hard to take good pictures. Then, in 1885, George invented film on a roll, which made taking pictures much easier. Photographers loved film. Even so, only a few people could afford a camera.

Brownie Camera

George wanted everyone to take pictures. He said the camera should be as "common as a pencil." In 1900, he invented the Brownie camera. It was so small that even a child could hold it! Best of all, it was cheap, so lots of people bought one. People got so excited about taking photos that George's company could hardly keep up with the demand for the cameras.

George liked the letter "k" and decided to name his company Kodak. George treated his workers kindly. He shared with them the profits from his business. He bought life insurance for them. That way if a worker died, his or her family would get money. If a worker got hurt, George made sure he or she saw a doctor. When a person grew too old to work, George gave him or her a small sum of money each month until the person died. Kodak workers were the first in the United States to have such **benefits**.

By 1902, George was rich. He started free dental clinics for children and gave money to schools with African American students. He wanted to help African Americans attend college. He said that educated workers were the best kind. He donated money to start a hospital, too. When George died in 1932, he left his fortune to the University of Rochester.

Now, even cell phones can take photos. It all started with George. He realized that we all want to take photographs.

George Eastman Invents the Kodak Moment

Directions: Darken the best answer choice.

1. Why did George choose to name his business Kodak?
   - (A) It was the first letter of his first two inventions.
   - (B) His workers chose the name.
   - (C) It was his mother's maiden name.
   - (D) He liked the letter "k."

2. The word **benefits** means
   - (A) good wages.
   - (B) safety measures on the job.
   - (C) special payments given by an employer.
   - (D) good ideas.

3. What happened second?
   - (A) George invented film on a roll.
   - (B) George started his own business.
   - (C) George invented the Brownie camera.
   - (D) George made a machine that used dry plates for photography.

4. Since the Brownie camera didn't cost very much,
   - (A) a lot of people began to take photographs.
   - (B) George offered his workers benefits.
   - (C) George's mother had to take in boarders to make ends meet.
   - (D) it didn't have to be set up on three legs like larger cameras.

5. If he were alive today, George would be surprised that
   - (A) people still use tripods.
   - (B) people still enjoy taking photographs.
   - (C) some workers get benefits from their employers.
   - (D) cell phones can take photographs.

6. From the way George used his money, you can tell that he wanted people to
   - (A) own their own homes.
   - (B) get a good education.
   - (C) become rich and famous from taking photos.
   - (D) have a lot of children.

Mine Fires That Keep Burning

In the 1800s, factories used steam power. Coal was burned in huge furnaces. The fire's heat made water boil. The boiling water made steam. The steam drove the machines' engines.

Getting coal was not easy. Coal miners worked in bad conditions. Most worked ten hours a day. Few miners ever lived to be thirty-five years old. The company thought a trained mule that pulled the coal cars out of the mine was more valuable than a miner. Why? It was easier to hire a new miner than it was to train another mule. If a miner got hurt, the company took him home in a cart. His family tried to help him. Back then, workers had few rights. The men accepted the dangers as a fact of life.

Then, in 1884, the owners of the Black Diamond Mine cut the miners' pay. The men earned 60 cents for each ton of coal they mined. The pay dropped to 40 cents. The miners went on strike. They would not go into the mines. They did not dig out the coal. Each day that they were on strike it cost the company money. But the owners did not back down. Neither did the miners.

A few miners soaked wood in oil. They put the wood into the coal cars. They set the wood on fire. Then they gave the cars a big push. The cars rolled down the track. They went deep into the mine. The fire spread to the coal. Soon the whole mine was on fire.

These men had started the world's longest-burning fire. More than 125 years later, it still burns. The fire is called the Devil's Oven. It burns in the coal veins around New Straitsville, Ohio. In the 1930s, the fire was close to the surface. People cooked food over smoking holes in the ground. That's when the U.S. government sent a crew. The men tried hard to **extinguish** the fire. Nothing they did worked. Now the fire is burning about 40 feet below the ground. It has burned 276 million tons of coal so far.

Pennsylvania has a mine fire, too. It started in 1962. People burned trash. Sparks went into the air. They landed on a strip mine. (A strip mine takes coal from the ground's surface.) The fire spread into an underground mine. As it burned, it moved under the town of Centralia. The U.S. government paid the people living there to leave. People have tried many ways to put out the fire. But once a coal mine starts burning, it cannot be stopped. Experts say that this fire will burn for another 250 years.

Mine Fires That Keep Burning

In the 1800s, most factories used steam power. Coal was put into huge furnaces and set on fire. The fire's heat made water boil. The boiling water created steam. The steam drove the machines' engines.

Getting coal was not easy. Coal miners worked in tough conditions. Most miners worked at least ten hours a day. Their work was so dangerous that few miners ever reached the age of thirty-five. The company viewed a trained mule that pulled the coal cars from the depths of the mine to the surface as more valuable than a miner. It was easier to find a man to replace a miner than it was to train another mule. If a miner was hurt in a mining accident, he did not get a doctor's care. The company took him home in a cart. His family did their best to take care of him. At this time, workers had few rights. The men accepted the dangers as a fact of life.

But then, in 1884, the owners of the Black Diamond Mine made a decision. They cut the miners' pay. Instead of earning 60 cents for each ton of coal they mined, the men would get just 40 cents. This made the miners mad. They went on strike. They would not go into the mines. They refused to dig out the coal. Each day that they stayed out of the mines it cost the company money. Even so, the owners did not back down. Neither did the miners.

Then, a few of the miners lost their tempers. They soaked wood in oil. They put the wood into several coal cars. They set the wood on fire. Then they pushed the heavy cars into the mine. The cars rolled down the track. They went deep into the mine. The fire spread to the coal in the walls of the mine. After a while, the whole mine was on fire.

The men who did this did not know that the fire they lit would outlive them. They had started the world's longest-burning fire. It is still burning more than 125 years later. This underground fire is called the Devil's Oven. It burns in the coal veins in New Straitsville, Ohio. In the 1930s, the fire came close to the surface. People cooked food over smoking holes in the ground. That's when the U.S. government sent a work crew. The crew tried hard to **extinguish** the fire. But nothing the men did worked. Today, the fire is burning about 40 feet underground. Devil's Oven has already burned 276 million tons of coal.

This is not the only mine fire. One in Pennsylvania has been burning since 1962. But that one started by accident. People were burning trash, and sparks landed on a nearby strip mine. (Strip mining removes coal from the ground's surface.) Soon the fire spread into an underground mine. As it burned, it moved under the town of Centralia. The U.S. government paid the people living in the town to leave. People have tried different methods to put out the fire. But once a coal mine starts burning, there is no way to stop it. Experts say that the fire beneath Centralia will burn for another 250 years.

Mine Fires That Keep Burning

In the 1800s, most factories used steam power. Coal was dug from the ground, put into huge furnaces, and set on fire. The fire's heat made water boil and created steam. The steam drove the machines' engines.

Getting coal was not easy. Coal miners worked in tough conditions. Most miners worked at least ten hours a day, and their work was so dangerous that few ever reached the age of thirty-five. The company thought a trained mule that pulled the coal cars from the depths of the mine to the surface was more valuable than a miner. It was easier to find a man to replace a miner than it was to train another mule. If a miner was hurt in a mining accident, he did not get a doctor's care. The company took him home in a cart. His family did their best to take care of him. At this time, workers had few rights, so the men accepted the dangers as a fact of life.

But then, in 1884, at the Black Diamond Mine, the owners decided to cut the miners' pay. Instead of getting 60 cents for each ton of coal they mined, the men would get just 40 cents. This made the miners so mad that they went on strike. They would not go into the mines and dig out the coal. Each day that they stayed out of the mines it cost the company money. Even so, the owners did not back down. Neither did the miners.

Then, a few of the miners lost their tempers. They soaked wood in oil and put it into coal cars. They set the wood on fire and pushed the heavy cars into the mine. The cars rolled down the track deep into the mine. The fire spread to the coal in the mine's walls. After a while, the whole mine was on fire.

The men who did this did not realize that the fire they lit would outlive them. They had started the world's longest-burning fire. It is still burning more than 125 years later. This underground fire is called the Devil's Oven. It burns in the coal veins in New Straitsville, Ohio. In the 1930s, the fire came close to the surface, and people cooked food over smoking holes in the ground. That's when the U.S. government sent a crew to **extinguish** the fire. But nothing the crew did worked. Today, the fire is burning about 40 feet below the ground. Devil's Oven has already burned 276 million tons of coal.

This is not the only mine fire. One in Pennsylvania that started by accident has been burning since 1962. People were burning trash, and sparks ignited a nearby strip mine. (Strip mining removes coal from the ground's surface.) Soon the fire spread into an underground mine. As it burned, it moved under the town of Centralia. The U.S. government paid the people living in the town to leave. People have tried different methods to put out the fire, but once a coal mine starts burning, there is no way to stop it. Experts say that the fire beneath Centralia will burn for another 250 years.

Mine Fires That Keep Burning

Directions: Darken the best answer choice.

1. When a coal miner got hurt in the 1800s,
   Ⓐ the mine owners rushed him to a doctor.
   Ⓑ he was taken to a hospital owned by the coal mine.
   Ⓒ he was given a trained mule.
   Ⓓ he was taken home.

2. The word **extinguish** means to
   Ⓐ put out.
   Ⓑ get under control.
   Ⓒ start.
   Ⓓ replace.

3. What happened second?
   Ⓐ The United States government made people leave a town in Pennsylvania.
   Ⓑ The United States government tried to put out a mine fire in Ohio.
   Ⓒ People burning trash started a mine fire in Pennsylvania.
   Ⓓ Coal miners started a mine fire in Ohio.

4. Why did coal miners set the Black Diamond Mine on fire?
   Ⓐ They wanted to be famous for starting the world's longest-burning fire.
   Ⓑ They thought it was a safer way to mine coal than traditional methods.
   Ⓒ They wanted to punish the mine's owners for cutting their pay.
   Ⓓ They were tired of working a dangerous job.

5. Why did the United States government pay people to leave Centralia, Pennsylvania?
   Ⓐ The town was destroyed by lava.
   Ⓑ The government was trying to improve the working conditions for coal miners.
   Ⓒ The government had discovered a valuable new coal mine beneath the town.
   Ⓓ There is a large fire burning beneath the whole town.

6. Why was coal so important during the 1800s?
   Ⓐ It was needed to make steam power.
   Ⓑ It was needed to power cars and trucks.
   Ⓒ It was used as part of machinery in factories.
   Ⓓ It was made into diamond jewelry.

Cold and Hot Deserts

Do you think that all deserts are hot and sandy? It's not true. There are hot deserts, cold deserts, and rain-shadow deserts. A desert can be stony, sandy, or icy. It can be flat. It can have mountains. How are all deserts alike? They are dry. Any water is deep under the ground.

Antarctica's cold desert is a hard place to live. It is always covered by ice and snow. There are high winds. Still, bacteria, algae, and moss live there. Penguins, seals, birds, and fish also live there.

Africa has the world's biggest desert. The Sahara Desert is part of twelve countries. During the day, it gets as hot as 105°F. Then it is freezing cold at night! Most of the world's deserts have this pattern.

The hot desert is a harsh place. Plants grow slowly. They have long roots. These roots seek out water. Few animals live there. They spend the day in holes. They stay under the ground. When the sun sets, they come out. They look for food.

There is a desert on every continent. Deserts can **increase** in size. How? People let their herds eat grass at the edges of the desert. The grass roots hold the dirt in place. When the roots are gone, the desert spreads into the new area. Then animals have less space to graze. This is a big problem in Africa.

A rain-shadow desert forms on one side of a mountain range. There is a big one in the United States. It covers 20 percent of the nation's land. This desert lies in parts of Washington, Oregon, and California. It is in parts of Idaho, Montana, Wyoming, Nevada, and Utah. It covers parts of Canada, too. It is called the high desert.

In the summer, the high desert is hot and dry. In the winter, it is cold. The spring may have flash floods. What causes this weather pattern? It's caused by the Sierra Nevada and the Cascade Mountains. They stand between the Pacific Ocean and the high desert. Rain clouds form over the sea. Winds move the clouds east. The clouds hit the west side of the tall mountains. They drop their rain. The rain does not make it to the other side of the mountains. The western side of these mountains has lush, green forests. The eastern side gets less than twenty inches of rain and snow each year. When rain does fall, it may fall fast. Then there's a flood. The ground cannot soak up the water fast enough.

The plants and animals that live in the high desert have adapted to these conditions. Ponderosa pine, bunchgrass, and shrubs live there. Lizards, great horned owls, and kangaroo rats are at home there, too.

Cold and Hot Deserts

Do you think that all deserts are hot and sandy? It's not true. There are hot deserts, cold deserts, and rain-shadow deserts. A desert can be stony, sandy, or icy. It can be flat or have mountains. What do all deserts have in common? They are very dry, and any water is beneath the ground.

Antarctica's cold desert is a tough place to survive. Ice and snow cover it all year. There are high winds. Still, tiny plants such as bacteria, algae, and moss live there. Penguins, seals, birds, and fish also live there.

Africa has the world's biggest desert. The Sahara Desert is so big that it crosses twelve countries. During the day, it gets as hot as 105°F. Then it gets freezing cold at night! Most of the deserts of the world follow this pattern.

The hot desert is a harsh environment. The plants that live there grow slowly. They have very long roots to seek out water. Few animals live in a hot desert. Those that do, spend their days in holes deep under the ground. They come out at night to look for food.

Every continent has at least one desert. Deserts can **increase** in size. How? People let their herds eat grass at the edges of the desert. The grass roots hold the dirt in place. When the roots are gone, the desert spreads into the new area. Then animals have less space to graze. This is causing trouble in Africa.

A rain-shadow desert is formed by a mountain range. There is a large one in the United States. It takes up 20 percent of the nation's land area. This desert lies in parts of Washington, Oregon, California, Idaho, Montana, Wyoming, Nevada, and Utah. It covers parts of Canada, too. It is called the high desert.

The high desert is hot and dry in the summer. In the winter, it is cold. The spring may bring flash floods. What causes this weird weather pattern? The Sierra Nevada and Cascade Mountain Ranges lie between the Pacific Ocean and the high desert. Winds carry rain clouds east from the sea. The clouds hit the west side of these mountains. They drop their rain. The rain does not make it to the other side of the mountains. The western side of these mountains  has lush, green forests. The eastern side gets less than twenty inches of rain and snow each year. When rain does fall, it can cause a flood. The ground cannot absorb the water fast enough.

The plants and animals that live in the high desert have adapted to these conditions. Ponderosa pines, bunchgrass, and shrubs live in this area. Lizards, great horned owls, and kangaroo rats make their homes there, too.

Cold and Hot Deserts

Do you think that all deserts are hot and sandy? It's not true. There are hot deserts, cold deserts, and rain-shadow deserts. A desert can be stony, sandy, or icy. It can be flat or mountainous. The only thing that all deserts have in common is that they are very dry and any water is far beneath the ground.

Antarctica's cold desert is a difficult place to survive. It is always covered by ice and snow and battered by high winds. Even so, tiny plants such as bacteria, algae, and moss live there. Penguins, seals, birds, and fish also live there.

Africa has the world's biggest desert. The Sahara Desert is so large that it crosses twelve countries. During the day, the temperature can reach 105°F, and then it drops to freezing at night! Most of Earth's deserts follow this pattern.

The hot desert is a harsh environment. The plants that live there grow slowly and have very long roots to seek out water. Few animals live in a hot desert. Those that do, spend their days in holes deep under the ground, coming out only at night to look for food.

Every continent has at least one desert. Deserts can **increase** in size if people let their herds eat grass at the edges of the desert. The grass roots hold the dirt in place. When the roots are gone, the desert spreads into the new area, leaving the herds with less space to graze. This is causing problems in Africa.

A mountain range can form a rain-shadow desert. There is such a large one in the United States that it takes up 20 percent of the nation's land area. This desert lies in parts of Washington, Oregon, California, Idaho, Montana, Wyoming, Nevada, and Utah. It covers parts of Canada, too. It is called the high desert.

The high desert is hot and dry in the summer and cold in the winter. The spring may bring flash floods. What causes this weird weather pattern? The Sierra Nevada and Cascade Mountain Ranges lie between the Pacific Ocean and the high desert. Winds carry rain clouds east from the sea. The clouds hit the west side of these mountains. They drop their rain. The rain never makes it to the other side of the mountains. The western side of these mountains has lush,  green forests. The eastern side gets less than twenty inches of rain and snow each year. When rain does fall, it can cause a flood. The ground cannot absorb the water fast enough.

The plants and animals that live in the high desert have adapted to these conditions. Ponderosa pines, bunchgrass, and shrubs live in this area. Lizards, great horned owls, and kangaroo rats make their homes there as well.

Cold and Hot Deserts

Directions: Darken the best answer choice.

1. All deserts are
   (A) covered in sand.
   (B) very hot during the day.
   (C) growing larger.
   (D) dry.

2. The word **increase** means to
   (A) get bigger.
   (B) get smaller.
   (C) stay the same.
   (D) change quickly.

3. What happens first?
   (A) Animals graze at the desert's edge.
   (B) The desert gets larger.
   (C) There are fewer places for animals to graze.
   (D) Without the grass's roots, the soil blows away.

4. How many states in the United States are a part of a rain-shadow desert?
   (A) three
   (B) five
   (C) eight
   (D) twenty

5. In a rain-shadow desert, you wouldn't likely see
   (A) tall trees.
   (B) frogs.
   (C) shrubs.
   (D) lizards.

6. A rain-shadow desert always lies
   (A) on single side of a mountain range.
   (B) in Michigan.
   (C) along an ocean coast.
   (D) between a mountain range and a cold desert.

Mighty Meteors

Have you ever seen a shooting star? Guess what? It wasn't really a shooting star. It was a falling meteor. It shot across the sky. Then it faded fast. Why? Most meteors do not contain metal. They burn up. They never make it to the ground.

Meteors are rocks in space. Millions come into our atmosphere each day. (Once a meteor has reached Earth from outer space, it is technically called a *meteorite*.) But almost none reach the ground. The chances of getting hit by a meteor are one in ten billion. A man was hit by one in Italy in 1650.

A meteor also hit a woman in 1954. She was on her couch. A metal object fell through her roof. It bounced off a table. It hit her leg. It weighed about ten pounds. It was hot. It was smoking. But she did not get hurt. Her leg was just bruised.

Metallic meteors do not burn up in Earth's atmosphere. So they are the only kind ever found. Our moon has no atmosphere. Meteors that come toward it do not burn up. Instead, they hit the moon. That's why it has so many dents in it.

One large meteor made a change in Earth's surface and climate. It fell 65 million years ago. It was six miles wide! It landed in the Yucatán Peninsula. That is in Mexico. The meteor left a crater. A crater is a hole. It was 185 miles wide! The meteor blew up when it hit. A big cloud of dust rose into the sky. The dust stayed there for years. It blocked the sun's heat. The Earth cooled down. Many people think that this killed the dinosaurs.

In Arizona, there is a huge, round dent in the ground. It's called Meteor Crater. A meteor that fell 50,000 years ago made it. About 25,000 years ago, a meteor crashed in Texas. It left a hole 175 yards wide. That is almost the length of two football fields! Now, most people don't know it is there. Over time, dirt and rocks filled in the hole. In both of these cases, the meteor fell apart when it hit.

In 2009, another meteor shot across the Texas sky. Hundreds of people saw it. Small pieces of it were found in a field. It fell south of Dallas. It did not make a crater.

Mighty Meteors

Have you ever wished on a shooting star? It wasn't really a shooting star. It was a falling meteor. It seemed to streak across the sky. Then it faded fast. Why? Most meteors do not contain metal. They burn up. They never reach the ground.

Meteors are rocks floating in space. Millions of them enter our atmosphere each day. (Once a meteor has reached Earth from outer space, it is technically called a *meteorite*.) But almost none reach the ground. The chances of you being hit by a meteor are one in ten billion. A man was hit by one in Italy in 1650.

A meteor also hit a woman in 1954. She was lying on a couch in her home. Suddenly, a large metal object fell through her roof. It bounced off a table. It hit her leg. It weighed about ten pounds. It was hot and smoking. But she did not get hurt. Her leg was just bruised.

Metallic meteors can survive the fiery entry into Earth's atmosphere. They are the only kind ever found. Our moon has no atmosphere. Meteors do not burn up as they approach it. They hit the moon. That's why it has so many dents in its surface.

One large meteor made a major change in Earth's surface and climate. It fell 65 million years ago. It was six miles wide! It landed in the Yucatán Peninsula. That is in Mexico. The meteor left a crater, or a hole. It was 185 miles wide! The meteor blew up when it struck. A big cloud of dust rose into the sky. The dust stayed in the atmosphere for years. It blocked the sun's heat. The Earth cooled quickly. Many people think that this is what killed the dinosaurs.

In Arizona, there is a huge, round dent in the ground. It's called Meteor Crater. A meteor that fell 50,000 years ago made it. About 25,000 years ago, a meteor crashed in Texas. It left a hole 175 yards wide. That is almost the length of two football fields! Now, the crater is barely visible. Most people don't even know it is there. Over the years, dirt and rocks have filled it in. The crater is now dotted with weeds. In both of these cases, the meteor fell apart on impact.

In 2009, another meteor streaked across the Texas sky. Hundreds of people saw it. Small pieces of it were found in a field about 70 miles south of Dallas. It did not make an impact crater.

Mighty Meteors

Have you ever made a wish on a shooting star? It wasn't really a shooting star. It was a falling meteor. It appeared to streak across the sky, and then it faded away. Why? Most meteors do not contain metal. They burn up fast. They never reach the ground.

Meteors are rocks floating in space. Millions of them enter Earth's atmosphere each day. (Once a meteor has reached Earth from outer space, it is technically called a *meteorite.*) But almost none reach the ground. The chances of you being hit by a meteor are about one in ten billion. A man was hit by one in Italy in 1650.

A meteor also hit a woman in 1954. She was lying on a couch in her home in Alabama. Suddenly, a large metal object crashed through her roof. It bounced off a table and hit her leg. It weighed about ten pounds. It was hot and smoking. But she was not hurt. Her leg was just bruised.

Metallic meteors can survive the fiery entry into our atmosphere. They are the only kind ever found on Earth's surface. Our moon doesn't have an atmosphere, so meteors do not burn up as they approach it. They smash into it. That's why you can see so many dents in the moon's surface.

One gigantic meteor made a big change in Earth's surface and climate. It fell 65 million years ago. It was, six miles wide! It landed in the Yucatán Peninsula in what is now Mexico. It left a crater 185 miles wide. The meteor itself blew up on impact. A huge cloud of dust rose into the sky. The dust stayed in the atmosphere for years. It caused Earth to cool quickly. Many people think that this is what killed the dinosaurs.

In Arizona, there is a huge, round dent in the ground. It's called Meteor Crater. A meteor that fell around 50,000 years ago caused it. And around 25,000 years ago, a meteor crashed in Texas. Most of it fell apart on impact. When the dust and rock settled, the meteor had made a crater about 175 yards wide— almost the length of two football fields. Today, the crater is barely visible. Most people don't even know it is there. Over the years, dirt and rocks have filled in the hole. The crater is now dotted with weeds and small brush. In both cases, the meteor itself was destroyed.

In 2009, a fiery meteor streaked across the Texas sky. Hundreds of people saw it fall. Small pieces of it were found in a field about 70 miles south of Dallas. It did not make an impact crater.

Mighty Meteors

Directions: Darken the best answer choice.

1. Meteor Crater is located in
   - Ⓐ Arizona.
   - Ⓑ Mexico.
   - Ⓒ Texas.
   - Ⓓ the Yucatán Peninsula.

2. The word **metallic** means made of
   - Ⓐ rock.
   - Ⓑ metal.
   - Ⓒ flames.
   - Ⓓ frozen water.

3. Which event happened last (most recently)?
   - Ⓐ A meteor made a huge hole in the surface of Arizona.
   - Ⓑ A meteor left a 175-yard-wide dent in the ground in Texas.
   - Ⓒ A meteor killed an Italian man.
   - Ⓓ A meteor changed Earth's temperature.

4. Meteors that do not contain metal
   - Ⓐ blow up when they hit the ground.
   - Ⓑ often strike people.
   - Ⓒ can make major dents in Earth's surface.
   - Ⓓ burn up in Earth's atmosphere.

5. More meteors hit our moon's surface than Earth's surface because the moon
   - Ⓐ is a bigger object.
   - Ⓑ has a magnetic pull.
   - Ⓒ has no atmosphere.
   - Ⓓ is in the same orbit as most meteors.

6. You are looking up at the night sky. Suddenly, you see a small flash of light. It lasts just a few seconds and then vanishes. You just saw a
   - Ⓐ falling star.
   - Ⓑ meteor burn up.
   - Ⓒ jet plane.
   - Ⓓ space shuttle.

The Life Cycle of a Pond

Picture a pond. Do you see a body of water with algae on its surface? Most ponds have algae floating on them. It is a food source for the animals that live in and near the pond.

What lives in a pond? If you thought of turtles, fish, and frogs, then you're right. Spotted salamanders live in the damp area around a pond. They have dark, moist skin with blue or yellow spots. They only come out at night. They breed in ponds. Their babies hatch in the water. Salamanders eat the worms, grubs, and bugs that live there as well.

Many animals rely on a pond. Toads lay their eggs in the water. Their babies start out as tadpoles, just as frog babies do. But toads grow up faster. Then they leave the pond and live the rest of their lives on land. Mosquitoes lay their eggs in ponds. Dragonflies eat the mosquitoes. Ducks rely on ponds for resting and for food. One duckling can eat up to 3,000 mosquitoes a day! Herons and snakes visit ponds to catch frogs.

Ponds change over time. It's called pond **succession**. First, a pond forms. It may be the result of a landslide that blocks a stream. Or people may use earthmovers to dig a pond to collect water and stop flooding. Sometimes a beaver will build a dam with sticks. The dam blocks a stream. This forms a pond. The beaver needs a pond for its home.

No matter how it forms, a pond will not last forever. The bottom slowly fills in with dead plants and soil. After about ten years, a pond becomes a swamp. A swamp has standing water filled with plant life (like cattails).

After about twenty-five years, where the pond once stood will be a marsh. It has spongy ground. After about fifty years, it will be a grassy meadow. Within one hundred years, a forest may stand there. The smaller the pond, the faster its succession.

Have you ever wondered what the difference is between a pond and a lake? You might guess that it is size. But the answer is depth. A pond is shallow. Sunlight can reach to its bottom. This lets plants grow there. Also, a pond's water is the same temperature at the top and at the bottom. A lake is deep. It does not have rooted plants on its bottom. No light can reach them. And it is colder in the depths of a lake than near its surface.

The Life Cycle of a Pond

Picture a pond in your mind. Do you see a body of water with algae growing on its surface? Most ponds have algae floating on them. It is an important food source for the animals that live in and near the pond.

What lives in a pond? If you thought of turtles, fish, and frogs, then you're right. Spotted salamanders live in the damp area around a pond. They have dark, moist skin with blue or yellow spots. They only come out at night. They breed in ponds, and their babies hatch in the water. Salamanders eat the worms, grubs, and insects that live there as well.

Many animals depend on a pond. Toads lay their eggs in a pond. Their babies start out as tadpoles, just like frog babies do. But toads develop much faster. Then they leave the pond and live the rest of their lives on land. Mosquitoes lay their eggs in ponds. Ducks rely on ponds for resting places and for food. One duckling can eat as many as 3,000 mosquitoes a day! Dragonflies eat the mosquitoes, too. Herons and snakes visit ponds to catch frogs.

Ponds change over time. It's called pond **succession**. First, a pond forms. It may develop as a result of a landslide that blocks a stream. Or people may use earthmovers to dig a pond to collect water and prevent flooding. Sometimes a beaver will build a dam to block a stream. This creates a pond. The beaver needs a pond for its home.

No matter how it forms, a pond will not exist forever. The bottom gradually fills in with dead plant matter and the dirt that rainwater carries in. After about a decade, a pond becomes a swamp. A swamp has standing water filled with plant life (such as cattails).

After about twenty-five years, where the pond once stood will be a marsh with spongy ground. After about fifty years, it will become a grassy meadow. Within a century, a forest may have begun. The smaller the pond, the faster its succession.

Have you ever wondered what the difference is between a pond and a lake? You might guess that the difference is size. But the answer is depth. A pond is so shallow that sunlight can reach to its bottom. This lets plants live on the bottom. Also, a pond's water is the same temperature at the top and at the bottom. A lake is too deep to have rooted plants on its bottom. No sunlight can reach them. And it is much colder in the depths of a lake than near its surface.

The Life Cycle of a Pond

Picture a pond in your mind. Do you see algae growing on its surface? Most ponds have algae floating on them. It is an essential food source for the animals that live in and near the pond.

What lives in a pond? If you thought of turtles, fish, and frogs, then you're right. Spotted salamanders live in the damp area around a pond and come out only at night. They have dark, moist skin with blue or yellow spots. They breed in ponds, and their babies hatch in the water. Salamanders eat the worms, grubs, and insects that live there as well.

Many animals depend on a pond. Toads lay their eggs in a pond because their babies start out as tadpoles, just as frog babies do. However, toads develop much faster. Then they leave the pond and live the rest of their lives on land. Mosquitoes lay their eggs in ponds. Dragonflies eat the mosquitoes, and ducks rely on them, too. One duckling can eat as many as 3,000 mosquitoes a day! Herons and snakes visit ponds to catch frogs.

Ponds change over time in a process called pond **succession**. First, a pond forms, perhaps as the result of a landslide that blocks a stream. It may be deliberately formed when people use earthmovers to dig a pond to collect water and prevent flooding. Sometimes a beaver will build a dam to block a stream. This creates the pond a beaver needs for its home.

No matter how it forms, a pond will not exist forever because the bottom gradually fills in with dead plant matter and soil. After about a decade, a pond becomes a swamp, a place with standing water filled with plant life (such as cattails).

After about twenty-five years, where the pond once stood will be a marsh with spongy ground. After about fifty years, it will evolve into a grassy meadow. Within a century, a forest may stand in the pond's place. The smaller the pond, the faster its succession.

Have you ever wondered what makes a pond different from a lake? You might guess that the difference is size, but the answer is depth. A pond is so shallow that sunlight can reach to its bottom. This lets plants live on the bottom. Also, a pond's water is the same temperature at the top and at the bottom. A lake is too deep to have rooted plants on its bottom because sunlight cannot reach them. And it is much colder in the depths of a lake than near its surface.

The Life Cycle of a Pond

Directions: Darken the best answer choice.

1. A heron goes to a pond to catch a
   - Ⓐ duck.
   - Ⓑ dragonfly.
   - Ⓒ turtle.
   - Ⓓ frog.

2. The word **succession** means a
   - Ⓐ body of freshwater.
   - Ⓑ disaster that changes Earth's surface.
   - Ⓒ series of events that take place in order.
   - Ⓓ man-made change to Earth's surface.

3. An area is now a swamp. If left alone, what will it become next?
   - Ⓐ a pond
   - Ⓑ a marsh
   - Ⓒ a forest
   - Ⓓ a meadow

4. Which animal does not live all of its life in or near a pond?
   - Ⓐ a toad
   - Ⓑ a frog
   - Ⓒ a turtle
   - Ⓓ a salamander

5. Which land environment is the wettest?
   - Ⓐ a forest
   - Ⓑ a marsh
   - Ⓒ a meadow
   - Ⓓ a swamp

6. If a body of water has the same temperature at its surface as it does at its floor, it is a(n)
   - Ⓐ lake.
   - Ⓑ pond.
   - Ⓒ inland sea.
   - Ⓓ ocean.

Eerie Earthquakes

Our Earth's crust is like an eggshell. The shell has cracks. The cracks are between huge pieces of rock. They are called tectonic plates. Below Earth's crust is another layer. It is melted rock. It is thick like pudding. The big plates float on it. They bump into each other. One may slip past the other. This can cause an earthquake. Then the ground shakes. Buildings may fall down. Large cracks may open in the ground.

Scientists measure the movement. They find out the quake's magnitude. The more the ground shakes, the higher the magnitude. People have kept records. So far, the strongest earthquake had a 9.5 **magnitude**. It was in Chile. It is a nation in South America. That quake occurred in May 1960. It was bad. But it wasn't the one where the most people died. That happened in 1556. It was in China. About 830,000 people died. Another deadly quake struck in 2004. It happened under the sea. It caused big waves. They hit Southeast Asia. More than 229,000 people died.

The biggest earthquake in American history took place in 1964. It was in Alaska. It had a 9.2 magnitude. Most of the United States' quakes are along a fault line in California. It is the San Andreas Fault. Two plates meet at this fault line. Each year they move about two inches. That's the speed that our toenails grow. But if one plate suddenly moves fast, watch out!

Just four U.S. states do not have earthquakes. These states are far from the edges of tectonic plates. They have no fault lines. The states are Florida, Iowa, North Dakota, and Wisconsin.

An earthquake is scary. But you can live through it. If you are inside, get under a table. Then things will fall on the table instead of you. If you can, go to an inside wall. An inner wall is stronger than an outer wall.

What if you're outside? Run away from buildings, trees, and power lines. Drop to the ground. Stay there until the shaking stops. Keep your head safe. Cover it with your arms.

Is there any way to tell that an earthquake is about to hit? Maybe. Some animals act strangely. They feel small vibrations better than we can. Deer, dogs, and rabbits will run away from the spot where the earthquake will start.

Other animals seem to sense what is coming, too. Horses do not go into the barn. If they are in the barn, they do not eat. Cockroaches run in circles. Fish in a pond or lake leap out of the water. They do it again and again. Birds do not perch. They want to be in the air when the earth moves.

Eerie Earthquakes

Our Earth's crust is like a large eggshell. It has cracks. The huge pieces of rock between the cracks are tectonic plates. Below Earth's crust is a layer of melted rock. It is like hot pudding. The plates float on this layer. They bump into each other. One may slip past the other. This can cause an earthquake. Then the ground shakes. Buildings and trees may fall down. Large cracks may open in the ground.

Scientists have instruments that measure the amount of movement. They figure out the quake's magnitude. The more the ground moves, the higher the **magnitude**. The strongest earthquake in recorded history had a magnitude of 9.5. It happened in Chile. It is a nation in South America. The quake occurred in May 1960. But that wasn't the deadliest one. That took place in China in 1556. About 830,000 people died. In 2004, an undersea earthquake happened in the Indian Ocean. It caused huge waves to hit Southeast Asia. More than 229,000 people died.

The biggest earthquake in American history took place in 1964. It was in Alaska. Its magnitude was 9.2. Much of the United States' tectonic plate activity is along California's San Andreas Fault. Two plates meet at this fault line. They move about two inches a year. That's the same speed that our toenails grow. But if one plate suddenly moves fast, watch out!

Just four states in the United States never have earthquakes. These states are far from the edges of tectonic plates. There are no fault lines in these states. They are Florida, Iowa, North Dakota, and Wisconsin.

Earthquakes are scary. But most people live through them. If you are indoors, get under a table. This way falling objects will hit the table above you. If you can, go to an inside wall. An inner wall is stronger than an outer wall of a building. It is less likely to crumble.

What if you're outdoors? Run away from buildings, trees, and power lines. Drop to the ground. Stay there until the shaking stops. Head injuries are bad. So cover your head with your arms.

Is there any way to tell that an earthquake is about to hit? Maybe. Some animals act strangely just before an earthquake. They can feel small vibrations better than we can. Deer, dogs, and rabbits will run away from the place that will be the epicenter. (That's the spot where the earthquake starts.)

Other animals seem to sense the coming disaster, too. Horses will not go into the barn. If they are inside the barn, they will not eat. Cockroaches run around in circles. Freshwater fish leap out of the water. They do it over and over again. Birds will fly around. They will not perch on anything. They want to be in the air when the earth shakes.

Eerie Earthquakes

Our Earth's crust is like a gigantic eggshell. The shell has cracks. The large pieces of rock between the cracks are called tectonic plates. There is a layer of melted rock beneath Earth's crust. It is like boiling hot pudding. The plates float on this layer. They bump into each other. Sometimes one slips past the other. This can cause an earthquake. During an earthquake, the ground shakes. Buildings and trees may fall down. Large cracks may open in the ground.

Scientists have instruments to measure the amount of movement. They assign a **magnitude**. The more the ground moves, the higher the magnitude. The strongest earthquake in recorded history had a magnitude of 9.5. It happened in Chile. That is a nation in South America. The quake occurred in May 1960. But that wasn't the deadliest quake. That took place in China in 1556. Around 830,000 people died. In 2004, an undersea earthquake happened in the Indian Ocean. It caused huge waves that hit Southeast Asia. More than 229,000 people died.

The biggest earthquake in American history took place in 1964. It was in Alaska. Its magnitude was 9.2. Much of the United States' tectonic plate activity occurs along California's San Andreas Fault, where two plates meet. These two plates move about two inches a year. That's the same speed that our toenails grow. When one plate suddenly moves fast, watch out!

Only four states in the United States have no detectable earthquakes. They are located very far from the edges of tectonic plates. These states are Florida, Iowa, North Dakota, and Wisconsin.

Earthquakes are scary. But most people live through them. If you are indoors, get under a table. This way falling objects will hit the table above you. If you can, go to an inside wall. An inner wall is stronger than an outer wall of a building. It probably won't crumble.

What if you're outdoors? Run away from buildings, trees, and power lines. Drop to the ground. Stay there until the shaking stops. Head injuries are dangerous. No matter where you are, cover your head and face with your arms and hands.

Is there any way to tell that an earthquake is about to hit? Maybe. Animals act strangely right before an earthquake. They can feel tiny vibrations better than humans can. Deer, dogs, and rabbits will run away from the epicenter. (The epicenter is the spot where the earthquake starts.)

Other animals seem to sense the coming disaster. Horses will not enter the barn. If they're inside the barn, they will not eat. Cockroaches scurry around in circles. Freshwater fish leap out of the water over and over again. Birds will fly around and not perch on anything. They want to be in flight when the earth shakes.

Eerie Earthquakes

Directions: Darken the best answer choice.

1. A tectonic plate is
   Ⓐ an underwater earthquake.
   Ⓑ Earth's melted rock layer.
   Ⓒ a huge piece of Earth's crust.
   Ⓓ a crack in the ground.

2. The word **magnitude** means
   Ⓐ location.
   Ⓑ cause.
   Ⓒ danger.
   Ⓓ strength.

3. According to the article, which of these earthquakes happened third?
   Ⓐ a 9.2-magnitude quake in North America
   Ⓑ a 9.5-magnitude quake in South America
   Ⓒ an undersea earthquake in Southeast Asia
   Ⓓ a quake in Asia that killed 830,000 people

4. One problem that earthquakes cannot cause is
   Ⓐ damage to buildings.
   Ⓑ tornadoes.
   Ⓒ flooding.
   Ⓓ deep cracks in the ground.

5. Which of these states may have occasional earthquakes?
   Ⓐ North Dakota
   Ⓑ Iowa
   Ⓒ Ohio
   Ⓓ Wisconsin

6. You are in school when an earthquake begins. You should
   Ⓐ get beneath your desk.
   Ⓑ run out into the hall.
   Ⓒ stay where you are.
   Ⓓ lie facedown on the floor in the aisle.

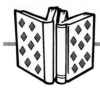

Pacific Northwest Native Americans

The Pacific Northwest Native Americans once lived in what is now Oregon and Washington. They lived in parts of Canada and Alaska. They ate elk, deer, and bears. They ate sea mammals. They got oil from fish. The oil was used to fry food. It was used as medicine, too.

The tribes used animal hides to make clothes. The women trimmed the clothes with porcupine quills. Both men and women wore earrings. They were made of sharks' teeth.

Many people think that a family is rich when it owns a lot of things. But the Pacific Northwest Native Americans did not. They said that those who gave away a lot were rich. Giving gifts was part of a party. This party was called a *potlatch*. Each guest got the same gift. Sometimes the family gave away blankets. Some gave red cedar baskets. Some even gave away canoes!

Potlatches were held for births, deaths, and marriages. At some, the hosting families would tell stories of their animal ancestors. Each family said it came from an eagle, wolf, raven, frog, or killer whale. If you were born into the frog clan, then that was part of your name. You wore the frog crest. You carved it on your bowls, forks, spoons, and totem pole. No one from outside the frog clan was allowed to use the frog crest.

A potlatch was held if a new totem pole was raised. The poles were made of red cedar logs. Each one stood in front of a home. The pole told each family's history. It had animals and spirits carved on it. People looked at the bottom of the pole most often. The clan chose its best artist to carve that part.

Music meant a lot to the people. They loved to sing. Each song was valued. Only the person who came up with a song could sing it! He or she could choose to let others sing it, too. There were special dances. The dancers wore shells on their clothes. The shells hit each other. They made music when the dancers moved.

Russians arrived on the Pacific Coast in 1741. They traded with the natives to get sea otter furs. The Russians took the furs back home. Everyone wanted them! So the Russians came back for more. The number of sea otters **dwindled**. The sea otter almost went extinct.

The Native Americans were in danger, too. Many caught Russian sicknesses. They had never had these sicknesses before. Thousands died from illness.

Pacific Northwest Native Americans

The Pacific Northwest Native Americans once lived along the Pacific Coast. They lived in what is now Oregon and Washington. They lived in parts of Canada and Alaska. They ate elk, deer, sea mammals, and bears. They got oil from the oolichan fish. It was used to fry food. It served as medicine, too.

The tribes used seal and walrus hides to make clothes. The women decorated the clothes with porcupine quills. Both men and women wore earrings. They were made of sharks' teeth.

Most cultures say a family is rich when it owns a lot. But the Pacific Northwest Native Americans did not. A rich family was one who could give away a lot. Giving gifts was part of a party called a *potlatch*. Each guest got the same gift. If one got a red cedar basket, they all did. Sometimes the family gave away blankets or even canoes! Families spent years making things to give away at a potlatch.

Potlatches were held for births, deaths, and marriages. At some potlatches, the hosting families would tell stories of their animal ancestors. In this culture, each family said it came from an eagle, wolf, raven, frog, or killer whale. If you were born into the frog clan, then that was part of your name. You wore the frog crest. You carved it on your bowls, forks, spoons, and totem pole. No one from outside the frog clan was allowed to use the frog crest.

A potlatch was held if a new totem pole was raised. Totem poles were carved from red cedar logs. They stood in front of the people's homes. The pole told the family's history. It had animals and spirits carved on it. People noticed the bottom of the pole most often. The clan chose its best artist to carve that part.

Music meant a lot to the people. They loved to sing. Each song was valuable. When a person created a song, only he or she could sing it! The owner could choose to let others sing it, too. Important meetings included dances. The dancers' clothing had shells. The shells hit each other and made music. The dancers moved to make the music.

Russians arrived on the Pacific Coast in 1741. They traded with the natives to get sea otter pelts. The Russians took the furs back home. Everyone wanted them! So the Russians came back for more. At first, both sides benefited by trading. But over time, the number of sea otters **dwindled**. The sea otter almost went extinct.

Even worse, the Native Americans caught Russian diseases. They had never been exposed to these sicknesses before. Thousands died from illness.

Pacific Northwest Native Americans

The Pacific Northwest Native Americans once lived along the Pacific Coast. They lived in what is now Oregon, Washington, Canada, and Alaska. They ate elk, deer, sea mammals, bears, and fish. Their most valuable food came from oolichan fish. Its oil was used to fry food and as a medicine.

The people made clothing from seal and walrus hides. The women decorated the clothes with porcupine quills. Both men and women wore sharks' teeth as earrings.

Most cultures think a family is rich when it owns many things. But the Pacific Northwest Native Americans had just the opposite view. A rich family was one who could give away all that it owned. This would be part of a party called a *potlatch*. Hundreds of red cedar baskets might be given away at one. Every guest got the same gift, whether it was a blanket or a canoe. Families spent years getting ready for a potlatch.

Potlatches were held in honor of births, deaths, and marriages. At some potlatches, the hosting families would tell stories of their animal ancestors. In the Pacific Northwest culture, each family believed it had descended from the wolf, eagle, raven, frog, or killer whale. If you were born into the frog clan, then that was part of your name. You wore the frog crest. You could carve it on your bowls, forks, spoons, and totem pole. No one from outside the frog clan was permitted to use the frog crest.

A potlatch was always given when a new totem pole was raised. Totem poles were carved from red cedar logs. They stood in front of the people's homes. Each pole told the family's history. They had animals and spirits carved on them. Since the bottom of the totem pole was the most visible part, the tribe chose its best artist to carve that part.

Music meant a lot to the people. When a person created a song, only he or she could sing it! The owner could allow others to sing it, too. Important meetings included dances. The dancers' outfits had shells. The shells hit each other and made the music for the dance.

Russians arrived on the Pacific Coast in 1741. They traded with the natives to get sea otter pelts. The Russians took these furs back home. Everyone wanted them! So the Russians came back for more pelts. At first, both sides benefited by trading. But then, the number of sea otters **dwindled** until they nearly became extinct.

Even worse, the Native Americans had no immunity for Russian diseases. They had never been exposed to these diseases before. Thousands of them died from illness.

Pacific Northwest Native Americans

Directions: Darken the best answer choice.

1. The Pacific Northwest Native Americans wore earrings made of
   - Ⓐ porcupine quills.
   - Ⓑ sharks' teeth.
   - Ⓒ hardened fish oil.
   - Ⓓ red cedar.

2. The word **dwindled** means
   - Ⓐ fell sick.
   - Ⓑ got larger.
   - Ⓒ got smaller.
   - Ⓓ left the area.

3. What happened first?
   - Ⓐ Many Pacific Northwest Native Americans died of Russian diseases.
   - Ⓑ The Russians took sea otter furs to their own nation.
   - Ⓒ The Russians wanted too many sea otter pelts.
   - Ⓓ The sea otter came close to dying out completely.

4. At a potlatch, the host always gave the guests
   - Ⓐ the same gifts.
   - Ⓑ gifts based on each person's status in the tribe.
   - Ⓒ in their same clan the best gifts.
   - Ⓓ clothing that had shells sewn on it.

5. You are a Pacific Northwest Native American who created a song. Who can sing this song?
   - Ⓐ just the members of your clan
   - Ⓑ just members of your immediate family (mother, father, brother, or sister)
   - Ⓒ just the leader of the tribe
   - Ⓓ just you and anyone to whom you give permission

6. You are a Pacific Northwest Native American who is part of the wolf clan. What do you carve on your doorposts and bowls?
   - Ⓐ a raven
   - Ⓑ a frog
   - Ⓒ a wolf
   - Ⓓ an eagle

The U.S. Constitution

Men from most of the thirteen colonies met in 1787. (Rhode Island did not send a man.) These men met to decide how the U.S. government would work. The meetings lasted four months. During that time, the men wrote the U.S. Constitution.

They split the government into three parts. Each had equal power. Why? The British king had too much power. The new Americans did not want one person or group to be too strong. So they set up three branches.

The legislative branch makes the nation's laws. The members of Congress make up this branch. Congress has two parts. They are the Senate and the House of Representatives. Each state picks two senators. The House of Representatives is bigger than the Senate. The number of members from each state is based on how many people live there. Some states send two people to the House. Some send two dozen.

The executive branch enforces the laws. The president leads this branch. He picks people for his cabinet. They help him. There are rules about who can run for president. The rules are in the Constitution. It can be a man or a woman. The person must be thirty-five years or older. He or she must be a natural-born citizen of the United States. He or she must have lived in the nation for at least fourteen years.

The judicial branch is made up of all of the nation's courts. The courts say what the laws mean. The highest court is the Supreme Court. It once had six judges. But that caused **deadlocks**. When the Court was split in half, they could not decide. Now there are nine judges. They are called justices. The chief justice is the head. Being picked for this court is a great honor. The judges are chosen for life. They can retire if they want.

The Constitution calls for "checks and balances." Each branch does its own job. It has some power to "check" the others, too. For example, Congress can pass a bill. But the president can veto it. Also, the president suggests a judge for the Supreme Court. The Senate can say "yes" or "no" to this choice. These are two ways the branches "check" each other.

Some people said the Constitution should tell the people's rights. So the Bill of Rights was added. This was in 1791. It has ten amendments, or additions. The Bill of Rights lists the rights of each American.

The U.S. Constitution

Men from most of the thirteen colonies met in 1787. (One colony did not send a man. It was Rhode Island.) These men met to decide how the government of the United States would work. The meetings lasted for four months. During that time, the men created the U.S. Constitution.

They split the government into three parts. Each had equal power. Why? The British king had used power against the colonists. The new Americans wanted to be sure that no part of the government got too strong. They did not want one person or group to run the whole country. So they set up the legislative, executive, and judicial branches.

The legislative branch makes the nation's laws. The members of Congress make up this branch. Congress has two parts. They are the Senate and the House of Representatives. Each state elects two senators. The House of Representatives is larger than the Senate. Each state sends elected officials based on how many people live in the state. Some states send two people. Others send two dozen.

The executive branch enforces the laws. The president leads this branch. He chooses people for his cabinet. They are his helpers. The Constitution has rules about who can run for president. It can be a man or a woman. The person must be at least thirty-five years old. The person must be a natural-born citizen of the United States. He or she must have lived in the nation for at least fourteen years.

The judicial branch includes all of the nation's courts. The courts say what the laws mean. The highest court is the Supreme Court. At first it had six judges. But that caused **deadlocks**. When the Court was split in half, they could not decide. So now there are nine judges. They are called justices. The chief justice is the head. Being picked for this court is a great honor. The judges are chosen for life. If they want to, they can retire.

The Constitution's writers created "checks and balances." Each branch does its own job. It has some power to "check" the other branches, too. For example, Congress can pass a bill. But the president can veto it. This is one way in which the branches "check" each other. The president suggests a judge for the Supreme Court. The Senate can agree or disagree with the choice. This is another way in which the branches "check" each other.

Some people said the Constitution should tell the people's rights. So the Bill of Rights was added. This was in 1791. It has ten amendments, or additions, to the Constitution. The Bill of Rights lists the rights of each American.

The U.S. Constitution

Men from most of the thirteen colonies met in 1787. (Rhode Island was the only colony that didn't send a man.) These men met to determine how the government of the United States would function. Their meetings lasted for four months. During that time, the men created the United States Constitution. It is an important document.

They split the government into three parts. Each one had equal power. Why? The British king had used power against the colonists. The new Americans wanted to be certain that no branch of government got too strong. They did not want one person or group to run the whole country. So they set up the legislative, executive, and judicial branches.

The legislative branch makes the nation's laws. The members of Congress make up this branch. Congress is made of the Senate and the House of Representatives. Each state elects two senators. For the House of Representatives, each state sends elected officials based on how many people live in the state. Therefore, some states send two people, and others send two dozen.

The executive branch enforces the laws. The president heads this branch. He chooses people for his cabinet to be his helpers. The Constitution has rules about who can run for president. The man or woman must be at least thirty-five years old and a natural-born citizen of the United States. He or she must have lived in the nation for at least fourteen years.

The judicial branch includes all of the nation's courts. The courts decide what the laws mean. The Supreme Court is the highest court in the country. At first it had six judges, but that caused **deadlocks**. When the court was split in half, they could not decide. So now there are nine judges called justices. Being selected to sit on this Court is an honor. The justices can serve for the rest of their lives, or they can retire.

The Constitution's writers created "checks and balances." Each branch does its own job and has some power to "check" the other branches, too. For example, Congress can pass a bill. But the president can veto it. This is one way in which the branches "check" each other. The president suggests a judge for the Supreme Court. The Senate can agree or disagree with the choice. This is another way in which the branches "check" each other.

Some people wanted the Constitution to detail the people's rights. They were afraid the government could mistreat its citizens. So the Bill of Rights was added in 1791. It has ten amendments, or additions, to the Constitution. The Bill of Rights specifies the rights of each American.

The U.S. Constitution

Directions: Darken the best answer choice.

1. The United States government has
   (A) one branch.
   (B) two branches.
   (C) three branches.
   (D) four branches.

2. When the U.S. Supreme Court had **deadlocks**, it meant that
   (A) all of the judges agreed on a decision.
   (B) decisions could not be made because the Court was evenly divided.
   (C) decisions were published in the newspaper.
   (D) the Court refused to hear a case.

3. What happened first?
   (A) A group of men met to write the United States Constitution.
   (B) The U.S. Supreme Court had six justices.
   (C) The U.S. Supreme Court had nine justices.
   (D) The Bill of Rights was written.

4. "Checks and balances" is a way to make sure that
   (A) people can make changes to the U.S. Constitution.
   (B) people have a specific set of rights that protect them from those in power.
   (C) the Supreme Court cannot have deadlocks.
   (D) one part of the government never gets too much power.

5. You have an idea for a new law that would affect the whole nation. Whom should you tell?
   (A) the U.S. president
   (B) your congressman or congresswoman
   (C) a Supreme Court justice
   (D) a local police officer

6. The U.S. president must
   (A) be a man.
   (B) be fifty years old or older.
   (C) have been born outside of the United States.
   (D) have lived on United States' soil for fourteen years or more.

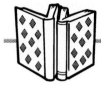

The Bill of Rights

The Bill of Rights is a document. It was written in 1791. It was added to the U.S. Constitution. It made ten additions. They are called amendments. Why? People did not think that the Constitution kept citizens safe from the government. The British King George had **abused** the colonists. That is why they went to war. Now they were free. They did not want to be mistreated again. The Bill of Rights lists Americans' rights.

The First Amendment says that you can have any faith. Or if you want, you can have no faith. You can say that the government is bad. You can disagree with leaders in speech and in print. Newspapers can pick what to print. You and others can meet. You can talk about things that you think are wrong. You can talk about changing laws. You do not have to be afraid. The government cannot stop you. In many nations, saying something against the government or the leader can put a person in jail.

The Second Amendment says that adults can have guns. They have the right to defend themselves.

The Third says that troops cannot live in your home unless there is a war. Then they can if Congress says so.

The Fourth says that your home cannot be searched. You cannot be stopped on the street to be searched. But if a judge says that there is a good reason to do so, then the search can take place.

The next four amendments protect you if you are accused of a crime. First, you must have a trial. The jury must be made up of your peers. Peers are people like you. The trial must be public, too. You do not have to speak at your own trial. You cannot be tried twice for the same crime. And even if you do a bad crime, no one can torture you.

Also, the government cannot just take what you own. It must pay you. So if the government wants to tear down your home to build a park, it must pay you for your house. It must pay you what it is worth.

The Ninth and Tenth Amendments say that you may have more rights than those listed in the Bill of Rights. You cannot have fewer. But you may have more. Also, each state government can make laws about things that the Constitution does not cover.

The Bill of Rights

The Bill of Rights is a document that was added to the U.S. Constitution in 1791. It has the first ten amendments, or additions. Why was the Constitution changed? People were worried. They did not think that it protected citizens from the government. The British King George had **abused** the colonists. That is why they went to war to win their freedom. They did not want to be mistreated again. The Bill of Rights is a set of laws that tells how the government can treat a person.

The First Amendment states that you can follow any religion. Or if you want, you can have no religion. You can say that the government or leader is wrong. You can disagree with leaders in speech and in print. Newspapers can pick what to print. You and others can hold meetings. You can talk about ways to change laws or the government. You do not have to be scared. No one can stop you. Today, in many nations, saying something bad about the government or the leader can put a person in jail.

The Second Amendment says that adults can own and carry guns. They have the right to defend themselves.

The Third says that you don't have to let troops live in your home unless there is a war. Then you may have to if Congress says so.

The Fourth says that you cannot have your home searched. You cannot be stopped on the street to have your body searched. But if a judge says that there is a good reason to do so, then the search can take place.

The Fifth through Eighth Amendments protect you if you are accused of a crime. First, you must have a trial. The jury must be made up of your peers. Peers are other people like you. The trial has to be public, too. You do not have to speak at your own trial. You cannot be tried twice for the same crime. And even if you are found guilty of a bad crime, no one can torture you.

Also, the government cannot take what you own without paying you. So if the government wants to tear down your home to build a park, it must pay you for your house. It must pay you what it is worth.

The Ninth and Tenth Amendments say that you may have more rights than those listed in the Bill of Rights. You cannot have fewer. But you may have more. Also, each state government can make laws about things that the Constitution does not cover.

The Bill of Rights

The Bill of Rights is a document that was added to the U.S. Constitution in 1791. It has the first ten amendments, or additions. The Constitution was changed because some people were worried. They did not think that it made the government protect its citizens. The British King George had **abused** the colonists, which is why they went to war to win their freedom. They did not want to be mistreated again. The Bill of Rights is a set of laws that tells how the government can treat a person.

The First Amendment states that you can follow any religion, if you prefer, you can have no religion. You can say that the government or leader is wrong in speech and in print. Newspapers can choose what to print. You and others can hold meetings to talk about changing laws or the government. You do not have to be afraid. The government will not stop you. Even now, in many nations, saying something bad about the government or a leader can put a person in prison.

The Second Amendment says that adults can own and carry guns. They have the right to defend themselves.

The Third says that you don't have to let troops live in your home unless there is a war. Then you may have to if Congress orders it.

The Fourth says that you cannot have your home searched. You cannot be stopped on the street to have your body searched, either. However, if a judge says that there is a good reason to do so, then the search can take place.

The Fifth through Eighth Amendments protect you if you are accused of a crime. First, you must have a trial. The jury must be made up of your peers—other people like you. The trial has to be public, too, instead of done in secret. You do not have to speak at your own trial, and you cannot be tried twice for the same crime. Even if you are found guilty of a bad crime, no one can torture you.

Also, the government cannot take what you own without paying you for it. So if the government wants to tear down your home to build a park, it must pay you what your house is worth.

The Ninth and Tenth Amendments say that you may have more rights than those listed in the Bill of Rights. You cannot have fewer, but you may have more. Also, each state government can pass laws about anything that the Constitution does not address.

The Bill of Rights

Directions: Darken the best answer choice.

1. The Fourth Amendment states that
   - Ⓐ adults can own guns.
   - Ⓑ you have the right to a fair, public trial.
   - Ⓒ you can practice any religion.
   - Ⓓ no one can search your home unless a judge thinks there is a good reason to do so.

2. The word **abused** means
   - Ⓐ ignored.
   - Ⓑ mistreated.
   - Ⓒ helped.
   - Ⓓ liked.

3. What happened second?
   - Ⓐ Americans wrote the Bill of Rights.
   - Ⓑ The British king angered the colonists.
   - Ⓒ The colonists fought in the American Revolution.
   - Ⓓ Americans wrote the U.S. Constitution.

4. The state government wants to tear down your house to build a highway bridge. What must the government do?
   - Ⓐ let you own the bridge
   - Ⓑ pay you what your house is worth in the local housing market
   - Ⓒ let you collect tolls from anyone who drives over the bridge
   - Ⓓ move your house to another piece of land

5. The Bill of Rights promises that you have the right to
   - Ⓐ disagree with leaders in public.
   - Ⓑ own pets.
   - Ⓒ get the best medical care.
   - Ⓓ join the armed forces.

6. You can be forced to
   - Ⓐ speak at your trial.
   - Ⓑ have a faith or religion.
   - Ⓒ own a gun.
   - Ⓓ go to jail if you are found guilty of a crime.

Oral Lee Brown Opens the Door

Oral Lee Brown is an African American woman. She was born in the early 1940s. She lived in the South. Her family was poor. Brown went to school and worked hard. She became a real estate agent, which means that she helped people to sell homes. She helped them to buy homes, too. Brown moved to California. One day in 1987, she was in a store. A young girl asked her for 25 cents. She needed it to buy bread. Brown wondered why the child was not in school. She could not stop thinking about her.

Brown was not rich, but she wanted to help the child. She went to a school to look for her. It was in East Oakland. The students there were poor. Just one out of four children there finished high school. Brown was led to a first-grade class. She did not find the girl. But she told the whole class that she would pay for them to go to college! At that time, she did not have the funds to make it happen. But she knew that she could work hard. She would save her money. She would keep her promise.

Brown made friends with each student. She listened to them. She gave advice. If they needed it, she gave them food and clothes. Their lives were hard. Sometimes she cried with them.

Each year, Brown saved $10,000 of her own money. She struggled to do it. Then she started the Oral Lee Brown Foundation. People gave cash to help. Nineteen of the twenty-three children finished high school. One became a firefighter. Another died. The rest went to college. Most were the first in their families to get a college degree.

Oral Lee Brown

Then, in 2001, Brown made the same promise to three more classes! Those students were in the first, fifth, and ninth grades. She did it again in 2005 and 2009. Now the Oral Lee Brown Foundation adopts a new group every four years.

Not every child will **succeed**. But Brown has given each one the chance. She tells them, "I have opened the door for you. You're either going to go through it or sit and look at the door. You must choose to make your life better." The good news is that most of the students walk through the door.

Oral Lee Brown Opens the Door

Oral Lee Brown is an African American woman born in the early 1940s. She lived in the South. Her family was very poor. She went to school and worked hard. She grew up to be a real estate agent. That means that she helped people to buy and sell their homes. Brown moved to California. One day in 1987, she was in a store. A young girl asked her for a quarter. She needed it to have enough money to buy bread. Brown wondered why the child wasn't in school. She could not stop thinking about the little girl.

Although Brown was not rich, she longed to help the child. She went to an elementary school to look for her. It was in East Oakland, California. The students there were very poor. In this school, just one out of four children completed high school. Brown was led to a first-grade classroom. She did not find the girl. But she told the whole first-grade class that she would pay for them to go to college! At that time, she did not have the money to keep her promise. But she was not worried. She knew that if she kept working hard and saving her money, she could do it.

Brown found that just making the promise was not enough. She made friends with each student. She listened to their problems and gave advice. If they needed help, she gave them food and clothes. Their lives were so hard that sometimes she cried with them.

Each year, Brown put away $10,000 of her own money. She struggled to save it. Then she started the Oral Lee Brown Foundation. People gave money to help. Nineteen of the twenty-three children finished high school. One became a firefighter, and another died. Seventeen went to college. Most of them were the first in their families to earn a college degree.

Then, in 2001, Brown made the same promise to three more classes! Those students were in the first, fifth, and ninth grades. She did it again in 2005 and 2009. Now, every four years, the Oral Lee Brown Foundation adopts a new group.

Oral Lee Brown

Not every student will **succeed**. But Brown has given each one the chance. She tells them, "Look, I have opened the door for you. You're either going to go through it or sit and look at the door. You must choose to make your life better." The good news is that most of the students walk through the door.

Oral Lee Brown Opens the Door

Oral Lee Brown is an African American woman born in the early 1940s. She lived in poverty in the South. She went to school, worked hard, and became a real estate agent. This means that she helped people to buy and sell their homes. Brown moved to California. One day in 1987, she was in a store when a little girl asked her for a quarter in order to buy a loaf of bread. Brown wondered why the child wasn't in school. She kept thinking about her.

Brown was not wealthy, but she wanted to help the child. She went to an elementary school in East Oakland, California, to look for her. The students there were very poor. In this school, just one out of four children finished high school. Brown was led to a first-grade classroom, but she did not find the girl. Instead, she told the first-grade class that she would pay for each of them to attend college! At that time, she did not have the money to make it happen. Yet she was not worried. She knew that by working hard and saving her money, she would keep her promise.

Brown soon found that just making the promise was not enough. She made friends with each student. She listened to their problems and gave advice. If they needed help, she gave them food and clothing. Their lives were so difficult that sometimes she cried with them.

Each year, Brown struggled to put away $10,000 of her own money. Then she started the Oral Lee Brown Foundation. People gave money to help her. Nineteen of the twenty-three children finished high school. One became a firefighter, and another one died. Seventeen students went to college. Most were the first in their families to earn a college degree.

Oral Lee Brown

Then, in 2001, Brown made the same promise to three more classes! Those students were in the first, fifth, and ninth grades. She did it again in 2005 and 2009. Now, every four years, the Oral Lee Brown Foundation adopts a new group.

Although not every student will **succeed**, Brown has given each one the opportunity. She tells them, "Look, I have opened the door for you. You're either going to go through it or sit and look at the door. You must choose to make your life better." The good news is that most of the students walk through the door.

Oral Lee Brown Opens the Door

Directions: Darken the best answer choice.

1. In her job as a real estate agent, Oral Lee Brown helps people to
   Ⓐ learn how to drive.
   Ⓑ buy or sell homes.
   Ⓒ go to college.
   Ⓓ find good jobs.

2. The word **succeed** means to
   Ⓐ graduate.
   Ⓑ agree.
   Ⓒ fail.
   Ⓓ do well.

3. Oral Lee Brown made the promise for the second time in
   Ⓐ 1987.
   Ⓑ 2001.
   Ⓒ 2005.
   Ⓓ 2009.

4. It is clear that Oral Lee Brown wants students to
   Ⓐ give money to good causes.
   Ⓑ have better health care.
   Ⓒ get college degrees.
   Ⓓ start their own businesses.

5. Which statement is true?
   Ⓐ People give money to the Oral Lee Brown Foundation.
   Ⓑ Brown has lived in the same state all of her life.
   Ⓒ Brown had the money to keep her promise to the students on the day she made it.
   Ⓓ Brown found the little girl she wanted to find.

6. Four of the students in the original East Oakland first-grade class
   Ⓐ became firefighters.
   Ⓑ died during their high school years.
   Ⓒ did not finish high school.
   Ⓓ finished high school but didn't go to college.

Condoleezza Rice, Former U.S. Secretary of State

Condoleezza Rice was born in 1954. She lived in Birmingham. It is a city in Alabama. Back then, it was the most **segregated** city in the U.S. This means that African American children did not go to school with white children. They did not use the same public restrooms. They did not drink from the same fountains. They had to sit in the back of buses. African Americans and white people could not marry.

Rice is African American. Her parents were proud of their only child. They would not let society hold her back. They paid for her to have private lessons. Rice learned to play the piano. She was a ballet dancer. She was an ice skater. She learned to speak French and Russian.

When Rice was eight years old, something awful occurred in her city. The Ku Klux Klan hid a bomb in an African American church. When it went off, the church was full. Two dozen people got hurt. Four girls died. One girl had been Rice's friend. Americans were upset. They wanted things to change. In 1964, the Civil Rights Act became a law. It said no one could keep people apart in public places due to their skin color. This law made it easier for African Americans to vote, too.

When Rice was ten years old, her parents took her to Washington, D.C. They went to the White House. But they did not go in. They stood at the fence. Rice told them, "One day, I will work there." Her parents agreed. They told her to set her sights high.

Condoleezza Rice

Rice went to college when she was just fifteen years old. She earned a doctorate degree. She taught at Stanford University. Rice won an award. It was for teaching. Then, she acted as the college's provost for six years. A provost is a college's second-highest leader. She managed a lot of people. She was the youngest provost ever. She was the first woman. And she was the first African American to have the post. She did her job well.

Rice became the U.S. Secretary of State. This was in 2005. She was the first African American woman to do so. In this role, she was in charge of U.S. diplomats. A diplomat is a person who lives in another nation. This person represents the U.S. in a foreign land. Rice moved diplomats to where they were most needed. She made them be experts in two regions. They had to speak two foreign languages. All diplomats had to live for a while in hard places like Iraq.

Rice worked with leaders of other countries, too. She helped them find ways to help themselves. Rice left when a new U.S. president took over.

Condoleezza Rice, Former U.S. Secretary of State

Condoleezza Rice was born in 1954. She lived in Birmingham, Alabama. At that time, it was the most **segregated** city in the U.S. This means that African American children could not go to school with white children. They had to use different public restrooms and water fountains. They had to sit in the back of buses. African Americans and white people could not get married.

Rice is African American. Rice's parents were proud of their only child. They did not want society to hold her back. They paid for her to have private lessons. She learned to be a pianist and a ballet dancer. She was an ice skater. She learned to speak French and Russian.

When Rice was eight years old, a tragedy occurred in her city. It shocked the nation. The Ku Klux Klan had hidden a bomb in an African American church. It went off when the church was full. Two dozen people were hurt. Four girls died. One of them was Rice's friend. It was a cruel act. It upset Americans. Their anger helped the Civil Rights Act of 1964 to become law. This law made it illegal to keep people separated in public places due to their skin color. It also made it easier for African Americans to vote.

When Rice was ten years old, her parents took her to Washington, D.C. They went to the White House but didn't go inside. They stood at the fence and looked at it. Rice told her parents, "One day, I will work there." Her parents said that they believed her. They told her to set her sights high.

Condoleezza Rice

Rice was so smart that she went to college when she was just fifteen years old. She earned a doctorate degree. She taught at Stanford University. Rice was a good teacher. She won an award. Then, for six years, she acted as the college's provost. A provost is a college's second-highest leader. She had a lot of people to manage. Rice was the youngest provost ever. She was the first woman. And she was the first African American to hold that post. Everyone agrees that she did the job well.

Rice became the U.S. Secretary of State in 2005. She was the first African American woman to do so. In this role, Rice made changes for U.S. diplomats. A diplomat is a person who lives in a foreign land and represents the U.S. She moved diplomats to the places where they were most needed. She required that they be experts in two regions. They had to be fluent in two foreign languages. All diplomats had to live for some time in hard places like Iraq.

Rice also worked with leaders of other countries. She helped them find ways to help themselves. Then they would rely less on U.S. financial aid. Rice left the position when a new U.S. president took over.

Condoleezza Rice, Former U.S. Secretary of State

Condoleezza Rice was born in 1954. She lived in Birmingham, Alabama. At that time, it was the most **segregated** city in the U.S. African American children could not go to the same schools as white children. They had to use different public water fountains and restrooms. They had to sit in the back of buses. African Americans and white people could not get married.

Rice is African American. Rice's parents were proud of their only child. They did not want society to hold her back. They paid for her to have private lessons in piano, ballet, and ice skating. She learned to speak French and Russian, too.

When Rice was eight years old, a tragedy occurred in her city that shocked the nation. The Ku Klux Klan had hidden a bomb in an African American church. It went off when the church was full. Two dozen people were hurt, and four girls died. One of them was Rice's friend. This cruel act upset Americans. Their anger helped the Civil Rights Act of 1964 to become law. This law made it illegal to separate people in public places based on their skin color, and it made it easier for African Americans to vote.

When Rice was ten years old, her parents took her to Washington, D.C. They went to the White House but didn't enter. They stood outside its fence and admired the building. Rice said, "One day, I will work there." Her parents said that they believed her, and they told her to set her sights high.

Condoleezza Rice

Rice was so bright that she entered college when she was just fifteen years old. She earned a doctorate degree. She taught at Stanford University. Rice was such a good teacher that she won an award. Then, for six years, she acted as the college's provost, which is a college's second-highest leader. She had a large budget and a lot of people to manage. Rice was the youngest provost ever. She was the first woman and the first African American to hold that post. Everyone agrees that she did the job well.

Rice became the U.S. Secretary of State in 2005. She was the first African American woman to do so. In this role, Rice was in charge of U.S. diplomats. A diplomat is a person who represents the U.S. while living in a foreign country. Rice moved diplomats to the places where they were most needed. She required that all diplomats be experts in two regions. They had to be fluent in two foreign languages as well. They all had to live for some time in difficult places like Iraq.

Rice also worked with leaders of other countries to help them find ways to help themselves. She wanted them to be more independent so they relied less on U.S. financial aid. Rice left the position when a new U.S. president took over.

Condoleezza Rice, Former U.S. Secretary of State

Directions: Darken the best answer choice.

1. In her role as U.S. Secretary of State, Rice
   (A) worked with foreign leaders.
   (B) created new international laws.
   (C) was in charge of the United States army.
   (D) managed people at Stanford University.

2. The word **segregated** means
   (A) poor.
   (B) unmarried.
   (C) separated by race.
   (D) rich.

3. What happened first?
   (A) The Civil Rights Act passed.
   (B) Rice went to college.
   (C) Rice visited Washington, D.C., for the first time.
   (D) A bomb blew up a church near where Rice lived.

4. Rice was the first African American woman to
   (A) serve as the provost at Stanford University.
   (B) teach at Stanford University.
   (C) be a United States diplomat.
   (D) run for vice president of the United States.

5. Think about the award that Rice won. You can tell that she
   (A) was the youngest person ever chosen to be the Stanford University provost.
   (B) was an excellent teacher.
   (C) went to college at an earlier age than most people do.
   (D) was the first female U.S. Secretary of State.

6. When Rice was growing up, she
   (A) could not go to school with white children.
   (B) was in a church when a bomb went off inside it.
   (C) did not take private lessons.
   (D) was the oldest child in a large family.

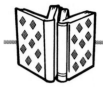

Guinea Pigs

May 15

Today, we stopped at the pet store. They had baby guinea pigs that were so cute! They were cuter than Joe's guinea pig because his has short hair. The ones I saw had long, curly hair. I asked Mom if I could have one. I begged and begged, but she said no.

On the way home, I kept pleading. She said that I had to read a book about guinea pigs. Then, if I still wanted to take care of one, she would buy me one for my birthday next week. I'm so excited! Tomorrow, I'll go to the library. Guinea pig, here I come!

May 16

I've been reading a book about guinea pigs. They are interesting animals. They have sharp teeth but rarely nip. They make squeaks when they are glad to see you, and they purr when you pet them! They need large cages to run around in. They eat timothy hay and pellets.

The book says that they do best when kept in pairs, but it warned to make sure they were both females or both males. Otherwise, you would have lots of babies. That sounds like fun to me, but I bet Mom wouldn't agree! I wonder if I can **persuade** her to get me a pair. I hope so!

May 18

I didn't write yesterday because I spent all my time reading about guinea pigs. They can't make their own vitamin C. They must eat fresh greens each day. Mom says we can get greens at the store each week. The pigs should be held a lot because it makes them friendlier. And they need a place to hide in their cage. That's where they sleep.

Guinea pigs are not pigs. In fact, they are not even like pigs. Someone started calling them "guinea pigs." It may be due to the noises they make. Or maybe it's because they like to eat all the time. They used to live in the wild in South America.

May 21

Today, I got a pair of sows! That is the name for female guinea pigs. Mom took me to a local rescue group where they had lots of adult guinea pigs. Their owners could no longer care for them. I got to pet many different ones. I held a lot of them, too. When I played with these girls, I knew they were meant to be mine. Their names are Mitzy and Hilda. We bought a really big cage, and I put it in the family room. I want to go play with them, so I will write more later.

Guinea Pigs

May 15

Today, we stopped in at the pet store, and they had baby guinea pigs there! I thought they were so cute! They were even cuter than Joe's guinea pig because his has short hair. The ones I saw had long, curly hair. I asked Mom if I could have one. Actually, I begged and begged, but she said no.

On the way home, I kept pleading. She said that I had to read a book about guinea pigs. Then, if I still wanted to take care of one, she would buy me one for my birthday next week. I'm so excited! Tomorrow, I'm going to the library. Guinea pig, here I come!

May 16

I got a book about guinea pigs. They are really interesting animals. They are one of the few pocket pets that rarely bite. They make squeaks when they are glad to see you and purr when you pet them! They need really big cages to run around in and lots of timothy hay and guinea pig pellets to eat.

The book says that they prefer to be kept in pairs because they are quite social. But it warned to make sure they were both females or both males, or you'd end up with lots and lots of babies. That sounds like fun to me, but I bet Mom would never agree. I wonder if I can **persuade** her to get me a pair of guinea pigs. I hope so!

May 18

I didn't write yesterday because I spent all my time reading about guinea pigs. They can't make their own vitamin C, so they need lots of fresh greens. Mom says we can get greens at the grocery store each week. The pigs should be held a lot because that makes them like people more. They need a place to hide in their cage. That's where they go to sleep.

Guinea pigs are not real pigs and are not even related to pigs. Because of the noises they make and the fact that they eat constantly, someone started calling them "guinea pigs." They used to run around wild in South America.

May 21

Today, I got a pair of sows! (That's what you call female guinea pigs.) Mom took me to a local rescue group. They had adult guinea pigs there whose owners could no longer take care of them. I got to pet and hold a lot of different ones. When I played with these girls, I just knew they were meant to be mine. Their names are Mitzy and Hilda. We bought a really big cage and put it in the family room. I want to go play with them, so I'll write more later.

Guinea Pigs

May 15

Today, we stopped at a pet store where they had baby guinea pigs! I thought they were so cute! They were even more adorable than Joe's guinea pig because his has short hair. These guinea pigs had long, curly hair. I asked Mom if I could have one. Actually, I begged and begged, but she said no.

On the way home, I kept pleading. She said that I had to read a book about guinea pigs, and then, if I still wanted to take care of one, she would buy me one for my birthday next week. I'm so excited! Tomorrow, I'm going to the library. Guinea pig, here I come!

May 16

I've been reading a book about guinea pigs. They are really interesting animals. They rarely bite, they make squeaks when they are glad to see you, and they purr when you pet them! They need gigantic cages to run around in and lots of timothy hay and guinea pig pellets to eat.

The book says that they prefer to be kept in pairs because they are quite social. But it warned to make sure they were both females or both males, or else you'd end up with lots of guinea pig babies. That sounds like great fun to me, but I bet Mom would disagree. I wonder if I can **persuade** her to get me a pair of guinea pigs. I hope so!

May 18

I didn't write yesterday because I spent my free time reading about guinea pigs. They can't make their own vitamin C, so they need plenty of fresh greens—but that's not a problem. Mom says we can get greens at the grocery store. They need a place to hide in their cage when they sleep, and they should be held often because that makes them sociable.

Guinea pigs are not actually pigs or even related to pigs. Based on the noises they make and the fact that they eat constantly, somebody started calling them "guinea pigs." They used to live in the wild in South America.

May 21

Today, I got a pair of sows! That's the name for female guinea pigs. Mom took me to a local rescue group that had adult guinea pigs whose owners couldn't care for them anymore. I got to pet and hold a lot of different ones. When I played with these girls, I just knew they were meant to be mine. Their names are Mitzy and Hilda. We bought a really large cage and put it in the family room. I want to go play with them, so I'll try to write more later.

Guinea Pigs

Directions: Darken the best answer choice.

1. A sow is the name of a
   - (A) kind of green vegetable that guinea pigs eat.
   - (B) baby guinea pig.
   - (C) male guinea pig.
   - (D) female guinea pig.

2. The word **persuade** means
   - (A) convince.
   - (B) worry.
   - (C) organize.
   - (D) threaten.

3. What happened first?
   - (A) The journal writer read a book about guinea pigs.
   - (B) The journal writer saw Joe's guinea pig.
   - (C) The journal writer played with guinea pigs at a rescue group.
   - (D) The journal writer saw guinea pigs with curly hair.

4. In the last journal entry, the writer
   - (A) decides not to get a guinea pig after all.
   - (B) buys a pair of baby guinea pigs.
   - (C) gets a pair of guinea pigs that will not have babies together.
   - (D) is given a breeding pair of guinea pigs that will have babies.

5. Why did the journal-writer's mother make him or her read a book?
   - (A) so he or she could learn how to find a book in the library
   - (B) so he or she would know how to take care of a pet
   - (C) so he or she would find out about different kinds of pets
   - (D) so he or she could find the name and address of a local rescue group

6. Guinea pigs originally came from a place that is to the
   - (A) east of the United States.
   - (B) west of the United States.
   - (C) north of the United States.
   - (D) south of the United States.

Dr. Seuss Loved Green Eggs and Ham

Do you like the Grinch? Most kids do. He is a character made up by Dr. Seuss. Seuss is one of the most popular children's authors of all time.

Seuss was born Theodor Seuss Geisel in 1904. He lived near a zoo. Seuss loved to go there. He dreamed of made-up animals and drew pictures of them. He gave them odd names.

Seuss went to college. He wrote for the school magazine. He drew **illustrations** for his articles, too. He drew a lot of cartoons. Then he took a job drawing cartoons at a magazine.

His first children's book came out in 1937. It was *And to Think That I Saw It on Mulberry Street*. But getting it into print was hard. Twenty-seven companies turned it down. They said it was weird because it was not like anything else on the market.

So how did Seuss get the book published? A college friend was an editor. He ran a children's press. Seuss ran into him. He told him about the trouble he was having. He said no one wanted his book. His friend said he would print the book. It was a big hit!

Theodor Seuss Geisel

Dr. Seuss never had children. But he loved kids. He wanted to write books that they would like. That way, kids would read them over and over. He did not want reading to be a chore. So he took 225 words from a list of 400 words. They were words that students know by the end of first grade. He used them to write *The Cat in the Hat*. It took him a year to write it.

The Caldecott Honor is the best award for a children's book illustrator. Three of his books won this prize. Seuss won a Pulitzer Prize, too. This award is given out each year. It is the best U.S. honor for any author. In 1991, Seuss was eighty-seven years old. He died in his sleep. He had made more than fifty books. They have sold more than 220 million copies. And guess what? They are still selling! Which of his books sells the most copies? *Green Eggs and Ham.*

Biography

Dr. Seuss Loved Green Eggs and Ham

Do you like the Grinch? Most kids do. He is a character created by Dr. Seuss. Seuss is one of the most popular children's authors of all time.

Seuss was born Theodor Seuss Geisel in 1904. He grew up in Massachusetts near a zoo. Seuss loved to go there. He thought about made-up animals. He would draw pictures of them and give them odd names. He had a great imagination.

Seuss went to college. He wrote for the school magazine. He drew **illustrations** for his articles, too. He drew a lot of cartoons. When he graduated, he got a job drawing cartoons at a magazine.

His first children's book, *And to Think That I Saw It on Mulberry Street*, was published in 1937. But getting it published was hard. Twenty-seven companies turned it down. They said it was too weird. It wasn't like anything anyone else had ever submitted.

How did Seuss get the book published? A college friend was the editor of a children's press. Seuss did not go to see him. He just ran into him. He told him about the trouble he was having getting his book out. His friend said he would print the book. His company was glad he did. It was a big hit!

Theodor Seuss Geisel

Dr. Seuss never had any children, but he loved kids. He wanted to write books that they would like to read. That way kids would read them over and over. He did not want reading to be a chore. So he took 225 words from a list of 400 words that students should know by the end of first grade. He used them to write *The Cat in the Hat*. It was so difficult that it took him a year to write it.

The biggest award for a children's book illustrator is the Caldecott Honor. Three of his books won this prize. In 1984, Seuss won a Pulitzer Prize, too. This award is given out each year. It is the highest U.S. honor for any author. In 1991, Seuss was eighty-seven years old. One day, he died in his sleep in his studio. He had made more than fifty books. They have sold more than 220 million copies. And guess what? They are still selling! Which is the most popular Dr. Seuss book of all time? *Green Eggs and Ham.*

Biography

Dr. Seuss Loved Green Eggs and Ham

Do you like the Grinch? Most kids do. He is a character created by Dr. Seuss, who is one of the most popular children's authors of all time.

Seuss was born Theodor Seuss Geisel in 1904. He grew up in Massachusetts. He lived near a zoo and loved to visit it. He thought about made-up animals and drew pictures of them. He gave them odd names. He had a great imagination.

Seuss went to college and wrote for the school magazine. He drew **illustrations** for his articles, too. He drew a lot of cartoons. When he graduated, he got a job drawing cartoons for a magazine.

His first children's book, *And to Think That I Saw It on Mulberry Street,* was published in 1937. But getting it published was difficult. Twenty-seven companies turned it down. They said it was too weird because it wasn't like anything anyone else had ever submitted. They didn't think people would buy it.

How did Seuss get his book published? A college friend was the editor of a children's press. Actually, Seuss did not go to see him; he just ran into him. He told him about the trouble he was having getting his book out. His friend said he would print the book. The company was glad because the book was a huge success!

Theodor Seuss Geisel

Dr. Seuss never had any children, but he loved kids. He wanted to write books that they would like to read. That way children would read them over and over. He did not want reading to be a chore. So he took 225 words from a list of 400 words that students should know by the end of first grade. He used them to write *The Cat in the Hat.* It was so difficult to do that it took him a year to write it.

The biggest award for a children's book illustrator is the Caldecott Honor. Three of Dr. Seuss's books won this prize. In 1984, Seuss won a Pulitzer Prize, too. This award is given out every year and is the highest U.S. honor for any author. In 1991, when Seuss was eighty-seven years old, he died in his sleep. He had created more than fifty books that have sold more than 220 million copies. And guess what? They are still selling! Which is the most popular Dr. Seuss book of all time? *Green Eggs and Ham.*

Dr. Seuss Loved Green Eggs and Ham

Directions: Darken the best answer choice.

1. What is the title of Dr. Seuss's first children's book?
   - (A) *And to Think That I Saw It on Mulberry Street*
   - (B) *The Grinch Who Stole Christmas*
   - (C) *Green Eggs and Ham*
   - (D) *The Cat in the Hat*

2. **Illustrations** are
   - (A) front covers of books.
   - (B) pictures.
   - (C) portraits of people.
   - (D) types of magazine articles.

3. What happened second?
   - (A) Seuss won his first Caldecott Honor Award.
   - (B) Twenty-seven publishers refused to print Seuss's first book.
   - (C) Seuss took a job drawing cartoons for a magazine.
   - (D) Seuss lived near a zoo.

4. You can tell that Dr. Seuss wanted to
   - (A) teach children a lot of new words.
   - (B) write books that children would read just once.
   - (C) create books where the pictures told the whole story.
   - (D) make reading fun for children.

5. Why did *The Cat in the Hat* sell so many copies?
   - (A) It was hard for Seuss to write it.
   - (B) It told a fun story using easy words.
   - (C) Seuss's own children appeared in ads to get people to buy the book.
   - (D) Most schools required that students read the book.

6. Where did Dr. Seuss get his pen name from?
   - (A) Seuss was his middle name.
   - (B) Seuss was his son's name.
   - (C) Seuss was the name of the town in Massachusetts where he grew up.
   - (D) Seuss was his favorite pet's name.

Delicious Discoveries

Joe Gregor didn't like making rolls. First, he measured the **ingredients**: flour, sugar, oil, water, and yeast. He mixed them together to form dough. Next, he kneaded the dough. Then, the dough had to rise. That took about an hour. At last, he split the dough into rolls. He put them into the oven. It took too long and had too many steps. But that was the only way to make rolls.

In 1949, Joe was a firefighter. He lived in Florida. One day, he was baking a pan of rolls. The fire bell rang. He took the rolls from the oven. He raced to the fire. After a few hours, the fire was put out. Joe went home. He saw the pan of cold, half-baked rolls. He decided to finish baking them. He wondered how they would turn out. He was shocked. They were delicious! Joe had just discovered brown-and-serve rolls. People buy millions of them each year. They are popular at Thanksgiving dinner.

Tea is a popular drink all over the world. The only thing that people drink more of each day is water. Tea is made through infusion. An infusion is when an object is boiled in water. It releases chemicals into the water. This changes the taste and the color of the water. Tea was discovered in 2737 BCE. Shen Nung was boiling water outdoors in China. Wind blew leaves from a bush into his open kettle. They infused the water. Shen Nung went to the kettle. He took the leaves out. Then, he tasted the solution. It was great! He had others try it, too. Almost everyone liked it. They wanted more. And that's still true. Last year, people drank more than 855 billion cups of tea.

In 1905, Frank Epperson was eleven years old. He lived in California. He used a wooden stick to mix soda powder and water in a glass. (Back then, this was a popular drink.) As he was stirring it, his mother called him inside. He forgot about his drink and left it on the porch. That night, it got very cold. The next day, he found his drink frozen. The stick had frozen in it. He pulled it out of the glass. He held it by the stick. He took it to school to show his friends. They took turns licking it. In 1924, Frank remembered his icy treat. He made and sold frozen soda water on a stick. First, he made his Epsicles in seven flavors. Then, he changed the name to Popsicle®. Last year, about three million of his treats were sold. Did you eat some of them?

Delicious Discoveries

Joe Gregor didn't like making rolls. First, he measured the **ingredients**: flour, sugar, oil, water, and yeast. He mixed them together to form dough. Next, he kneaded the dough. Then the dough had to rise. That took about one hour. At last, he split the dough into rolls and baked them in the oven. Joe felt it took too many steps and too much time. Yet that was the only way to make rolls.

In 1949, Joe was a firefighter. He lived in Florida. One day, while he was baking a pan of rolls, the fire siren rang. He took the rolls from the oven and raced to the fire. After several hours, the blaze ended, and Joe went home. He saw the pan of cold, half-baked rolls. He decided to finish baking them. He was shocked to find that they were delicious! Joe had just discovered brown-and-serve rolls. Now people buy millions of these rolls. They are popular at Thanksgiving.

Tea is a popular drink worldwide. The only thing that people drink more of each day is water. Tea is made through infusion. An infusion is when an object is boiled in water to make it release chemicals into the water. The taste and the color of the water changes. Tea was discovered in 2737 BCE. Shen Nung was boiling water in a kettle outdoors in China. Wind blew leaves from a bush into the open kettle. Before Shen Nung knew they were in the water, they infused the water. When he saw the leaves, he plucked

them out. He tasted the solution—and loved it! He had others try it, too. Almost everyone wanted more. And that's still true. People drank more than 855 billion cups of tea last year.

In 1905, Frank Epperson was eleven years old. He lived in California. He mixed soda powder and water in a glass using a wooden stick. (At that time, this was a popular drink.) As he was stirring it, his mother called him inside. He forgot about his drink and left it on the porch. That night, it got very cold. The next day, he found his drink frozen around the stick. He pulled it out of the glass. He took it to school. His friends took turns licking it—and liked it. In 1924, Frank remembered his icy treat. He made and sold soda water on a stick. First, he made his Epsicles in seven flavors. Then, he changed the name to Popsicle®. Last year, people bought about three million of his frozen treats. Did you eat some of them?

Delicious Discoveries

Joe Gregor didn't like making rolls. First, he measured the **ingredients**: flour, sugar, oil, water, and yeast, and then mixed them together to form dough. Next, he kneaded the dough. Then, the dough had to rise, which took about an hour. At last, he divided the dough into rolls and baked them in the oven. Joe felt it took too many steps and too much time. Yet that was the only way to make rolls.

In 1949, Joe was a firefighter in Florida. One day, while he was baking a pan of rolls, the fire siren rang. He took the rolls from the oven and raced to the fire. After several hours, the blaze was over. Joe went home and finished baking the pan of cold, half-baked rolls. He was shocked to find that they were delicious! Joe had just discovered brown-and-serve rolls. Now people buy millions every year. They are especially popular at Thanksgiving dinner.

Tea is a popular beverage worldwide. The only thing that people drink more of daily is water. Tea is made through infusion. An infusion is when an object is boiled in water to release chemicals, changing the taste and the color of the water. Shen Nung discovered tea in 2737 BCE. He was boiling water in an open kettle outdoors in China. Wind blew leaves into the open kettle. Before Shen Nung realized they were even there, they infused the water. When he saw the leaves, he plucked them out. Then, he tasted the solution—and loved it! He had others try it, too. Almost everyone wanted more. And that's still true: people drank more than 855 billion cups of tea last year.

In 1905, eleven-year-old Frank Epperson lived in California. He mixed soda powder and water in a glass using a wooden stick. (At that time, this was a popular drink.) As he stirred, his mother called him indoors, and he forgot about his drink. He left it on the porch, and it got so cold overnight that the next morning his drink had frozen around the stick. He pulled it out of the glass and took it to school to show his friends. They took turns licking it—and liked it. In 1924, Frank remembered this icy treat. He made and sold soda water on a stick. The first year he made his Epsicles in seven flavors. Then, he changed the name to Popsicle®. Last year, people bought approximately three million of his frozen treats. Did you eat some of them?

Delicious Discoveries

Directions: Darken the best answer choice.

1. Who discovered tea?
   - Ⓐ Frank Epperson
   - Ⓑ Joe Gregor
   - Ⓒ Shen Nung
   - Ⓓ The article does not say.

2. An **ingredient** is a
   - Ⓐ type of infusion.
   - Ⓑ part of a mixture.
   - Ⓒ frozen treat.
   - Ⓓ baking method.

3. Which of these discoveries was made last?
   - Ⓐ soda powder
   - Ⓑ tea
   - Ⓒ Popsicle® ice pops
   - Ⓓ brown-and-serve rolls

4. How many years passed between a boy's discovery of a frozen treat and the sale of the first Epsicle?
   - Ⓐ none
   - Ⓑ eleven
   - Ⓒ nineteen
   - Ⓓ twenty-four

5. During an infusion, both the taste and the color
   - Ⓐ move from leaves into water.
   - Ⓑ of Popsicle® ice pops are set.
   - Ⓒ of soda powder changes water into soda.
   - Ⓓ of brown-and-serve rolls is changed.

6. What would a person today be most apt to want on a hot day?
   - Ⓐ water mixed with soda powder
   - Ⓑ a brown-and-serve roll
   - Ⓒ hot tea
   - Ⓓ iced tea

Home   Story Samples   **Member Log In**

Beyond Belief

**Hundreds of TRUE Stories—So Amazing,
You'll Find Them Hard to Believe!**

The Cursed Crew

No one on board knew that they were about to make history when the *Mermaid* set sail. It left Sydney, Australia. The date was October 16, 1829. The crew set an incredible record. It still stands today. Four days out of port, their ship crashed onto a reef. It was in the Straits of Torres. On October 23, the *Swiftsure* picked up the whole crew. No one was lost. But on October 28, that ship ran aground. The whole crew had to abandon ship. Eight hours later, the men were saved. The *Governor Ready* picked them up. Just three hours later, that ship caught on fire. It was ruined.

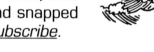

The schooner *Comet* was close by. It rushed to help them. So far, through all the wrecks, no one had died! Then, one week later, a storm struck. It ripped the sails and snapped the mast of the *Comet* . . . *to finish the story, <u>subscribe</u>.*

The Sweetheart Who Wouldn't Give Up

Merna loved Stan. He was a soldier in the Polish Army during World War I. She was told he was missing in action and probably dead. But she knew he was alive. She just didn't know where he was. Starting in October 1918, she had a dream. It came each night. She saw her beloved Stan. He was in a dark tunnel. He cried out for help. She went to the police. They thought she was **distraught** over the loss of her sweetheart. They said to forget about him. In July 1919, her dream changed. She saw an old castle on a hill. It looked like it had been bombed. As she got closer to the rubble, she heard Stan's cry for help. He seemed to be buried under the pile of rock. But could anyone be alive under that?

In March 1920, Merna started walking. She wanted to find the castle. She had no money. She slept under trees. She ate if people gave her food. On April 25, she came to the town of Zlota, Poland. She saw the castle from her dreams on the hill. She fell down . . . *to finish the story, <u>subscribe</u>.*

Visitor Number: 082607   Last Site Update: 04/02/11

Contact Us | Subscribe

Beyond Belief

Hundreds of TRUE Stories—So Amazing, You'll Find Them Hard to Believe!

The Cursed Crew

No one on the crew had any idea that they were about to make history as the *Mermaid* set sail. It left Sydney, Australia. The date was October 16, 1829. These sailors set an incredible record. Four days out of port, the ship wrecked. It crashed onto a reef in the Straits of Torres. On October 23, the *Swiftsure* picked up the entire crew. No one was lost. But on October 28, that ship ran aground. The whole crew abandoned ship. Eight hours later, the men were rescued. The *Governor Ready* took them aboard. Just three hours later, the ship caught fire. It was totally ruined.

The schooner *Comet* was nearby. It rushed to their aid. So far, through all the mishaps, no one had died! Then, seven days later, a squall struck. It ripped the sails and snapped the mast of the *Comet . . . to finish the story, <u>subscribe</u>.*

The Sweetheart Who Wouldn't Give Up

Merna loved Stan Omensky. He was a young soldier in the Polish Army during World War I. When she was told he was missing in action and probably dead, she refused to believe it. She knew he was alive. She just didn't know where he was. Starting in October 1918, she had a dream night after night. She saw her beloved Stan on his knees in a dark tunnel. He cried out for help. She went to the authorities. They thought she was just **distraught** over the loss of her sweetheart. They told her to

HELP!

forget about him. In July 1919, her dream changed. She saw a castle on a hill. Part of the castle had crumbled. It looked like it had been bombed. As she got close to the heap of rubble, she heard Stan's cry for help. He seemed to be buried beneath a pile of rock. But could anyone be alive under that?

In March 1920, Merna started out walking. She was determined to find the castle and end her nightmares. She had no money, so she ate only if people gave her food. On April 25, she came to the little town of Zlota, Poland. She saw the castle from her dreams on the hill. She collapsed . . . *to finish the story, <u>subscribe</u>.*

Visitor Number: 082607   **Last Site Update: 04/02/11**

Contact Us | Subscribe

Web Site

Home   Story Samples   **Member Log In**

Beyond Belief

Hundreds of TRUE Stories—So Amazing, You'll Find Them Hard to Believe!

The Cursed Crew

No one on the crew had any idea that they were about to make history as the *Mermaid* set sail from Sydney, Australia. On October 16, 1829, these sailors started an amazing journey that set an incredible record. Four days out of port, their ship wrecked on a reef in the Straits of Torres. On October 23, the *Swiftsure* picked up the entire crew. Not one man was lost. But on October 28, that ship ran aground, and the crew abandoned ship. Eight hours later, the men were picked up by the *Governor Ready*. Yet just three hours later, that ship caught fire and was completely destroyed.

The nearby schooner *Comet* rushed to their rescue. So far, through all the mishaps, no one had lost his life! Then, seven days later, a squall ripped the sails and snapped the mast of the *Comet . . . to finish the story, <u>subscribe</u>.*

The Sweetheart Who Wouldn't Give Up

Merna loved Stan Omensky. He was a soldier in the Polish Army during World War I. When she was told he was missing in action and probably dead, she refused to believe it. She knew he was alive; she just didn't know where he was. Starting in October 1918, she had a dream night after night of Stan on his knees in a dark tunnel, crying for help. Tormented, she went to the authorities for help. They thought she was just **distraught** over the loss of her sweetheart and ignored her. In July 1919, her dream changed. She saw a castle on a hill. Part of the castle was destroyed, probably from bombardment. When she reached the heap of rubble, she heard Stan's cry for help from beneath the pile of rock. But could anyone be alive under there?

In March 1920, Merna could bear the dreams no more. She had no money. She set out on foot to find the castle and end the nightmares. Merna slept under trees and ate only when people gave her food. On April 25, she came to the little town of Zlota, Poland. She saw the castle on the hill. It was the one from her dreams! She collapsed . . . *to finish the story, <u>subscribe</u>.*

Visitor Number: 082607   **Last Site Update: 04/02/11**

Contact Us | Subscribe

Beyond Belief

Directions: Darken the best answer choice.

1. From the details given, you know that the *Mermaid's* crew survived at least
   Ⓐ one shipwreck.
   Ⓑ three shipwrecks.
   Ⓒ five shipwrecks.
   Ⓓ seven shipwrecks.

2. The word **distraught** means
   Ⓐ very upset.
   Ⓑ confused.
   Ⓒ speechless.
   Ⓓ angry.

3. What happened last?
   Ⓐ Merna went to the police.
   Ⓑ Merna fell in love with Stan.
   Ⓒ Merna had bad dreams each night.
   Ⓓ Merna went to the town of Zlota.

4. The crew of the *Mermaid* is called "cursed" because they
   Ⓐ were being haunted by dead sailors.
   Ⓑ kept being involved in disasters at sea.
   Ⓒ had had a curse placed on them by a witch.
   Ⓓ didn't know how to sail a ship.

5. Why would a person subscribe to the Beyond Belief Web site?
   Ⓐ to finish reading the stories
   Ⓑ to write stories for the Web site
   Ⓒ to print the Beyond Belief stories in a magazine
   Ⓓ to win a prize

6. Look at the ship names in the first story. You can tell that a ship's name is printed in
   Ⓐ all lowercase letters.
   Ⓑ all uppercase letters.
   Ⓒ italics (slanted letters).
   Ⓓ boldface.

The River Times

The Miracle on the Hudson

January 15, 2009

NEW YORK (AP)—Make a note of this date. Today the world saw its first perfect emergency water landing of a jet plane. The plane landed in icy cold water. It went into the Hudson River in New York City. The plane was U.S. Airways Flight 1549. It left the Airport at 3:26 p.m. It was going to North Carolina. But as it took off, the jet hit a flock of geese. The birds flew into the engines. Both engines quit. The plane was doomed. It was going down.

The plane had been in the air less than one minute. The pilot called the tower. He reported a "double bird strike." He said that he had to return. The air traffic controller told the pilot no. Instead, he said to go to a nearby airport in New Jersey. It is not known why the plane was not allowed to return.

The plane lost **altitude** fast. The pilot knew it could not reach New Jersey. He did the only thing he could do. He landed in the Hudson River.

The pilot is Chesley "Sully" Sullenberger. He has flown gliders and jets for forty years. He guided the damaged plane into the water. He did it with such skill that it shocked those who saw it. The plane hit the water gently. It did not break apart. But it did start to sink. The people rushed to get out. They stood on the wings. They were knee-deep in the water. Some people fell or jumped into the water. The air was 20°F. The water was 36°F. That's just 4 degrees above freezing.

Coast Guard boats and a NY Waterway ferry were close by. They rushed to help. The passengers were in danger. If their body temperatures dropped too low, they could die. In the cold, it could take just five minutes for that to happen.

All 155 aboard survived the landing. In every other crash landing in water, the jet has broken apart. At least some of those onboard have died. Often, most of them died. But today, no one died. In fact, there were no bad injuries! One person did have two broken legs. A few were treated for being too cold. New York governor David Patterson called this "A Miracle on the Hudson."

The plane floated down the river. Rescue workers hauled it from the water. By then, just half of the tail fin could be seen. The rest of the plane had sunk. It had drifted four miles from where it had hit the water.

The River Times

The Miracle on the Hudson

January 15, 2009

NEW YORK (AP)—Make a note of this date. Today the world saw its first perfect emergency water landing of a jet plane. The plane plunged into icy cold water. It went into the Hudson River in New York City. It all started this afternoon. U.S. Airways Flight 1549 took off. It left LaGuardia Airport at 3:26 p.m. It was going to North Carolina. But as it rose from the ground, the jet hit a flock of geese. The birds flew into the engines. Both engines quit. The plane was doomed. It was going down.

Less than one minute into the flight, the pilot called the tower. He reported a "double bird strike." He said that he had to return. The air traffic controller told the pilot no. Instead, he said to go to a nearby airport. It is in New Jersey. It is not known why the request to return was turned down.

The plane lost **altitude** fast. The pilot knew it could not reach New Jersey. He did the only thing left to do. He landed in the Hudson River.

The pilot is Chesley "Sully" Sullenberger. He has a lot of experience. He has flown gliders and jets for forty years. He guided the disabled plane into the water. He did it with such skill that it shocked all those who watched it. The plane struck the water gently. It did not break apart. But it did start to sink. The passengers hurried to get out. They stood on the wings. They were knee-deep in the cold water. The air was 20°F. The water was 36°F. That's just 4 degrees above freezing.

Luckily, a NY Waterway ferry and Coast Guard boats were nearby. They rushed to get the passengers. At that point, the biggest danger was hypothermia. This occurs when the body's temperature drops too low. At such low temperatures, it could take just five minutes for hypothermia to set in. Police divers also got some of the passengers from the water.

The miracle was that all 155 aboard survived the crash landing. In every other crash landing in water, the jet has broken apart. At least some of those onboard have died. Too often, most of them died. In this case, not only did no one die, but there were no bad injuries! One person did have two broken legs. A few were treated for hypothermia. No wonder New York governor David Patterson has called this "A Miracle on the Hudson."

And what became of the plane? It floated down the river. Rescue workers hauled the plane from the river. By then, just half of the tail fin was still above water. The jet had drifted four miles from where it had entered the water.

The River Times

The Miracle on the Hudson

January 15, 2009

NEW YORK (AP)—Make a note of this date. Today the world saw its first successful emergency water landing of a jet plane. The plane plunged into the icy cold waters of the Hudson River in New York City. It all started this afternoon. U.S. Airways Flight 1549 took off from LaGuardia Airport at 3:26 p.m. It was going to North Carolina. But as it rose from the runway, the jet struck a flock of geese. The birds flew into the engines. Both engines quit. The plane was doomed. It was going down.

Less than one minute into the flight, the pilot reported a "double bird strike." He said that he had to return to LaGuardia. The air traffic controller told the pilot no. Instead, he said to go to a nearby airport in New Jersey. It is unknown at this time why the request to return was denied.

The plane lost **altitude** fast. The pilot knew it could not reach New Jersey. He did the only thing left to do: he landed in the Hudson River.

The pilot, Chesley "Sully" Sullenberger, is an experienced pilot. He has flown gliders and jets for forty years. He guided the disabled plane into the water with a skill that astounded all those who watched it. The plane struck the water gently. It did not break apart. But it did start to sink. The scared passengers scurried to get out. They stood on the wings. They were knee-deep in the cold river water. The air was 20°F. The water was 36°F. That's just 4 degrees above freezing.

Luckily, a NY Waterway ferry and Coast Guard boats were nearby in the river. They rushed to get the passengers. At that point, the biggest danger was hypothermia. Hypothermia occurs when the body's temperature drops too low. At such low temperatures, it could take just five minutes for

hypothermia to set in. Police divers did rescue some of the passengers from the water.

The miracle was that all 155 aboard survived the crash landing. In every other emergency landing in water, the jet has broken into pieces. At least some of the people onboard have died. Often, most of them died. In this instance, not only did no one die, but there were no serious injuries! One person did have two broken legs. Several were treated for hypothermia. No wonder New York governor David Patterson has called this "A Miracle on the Hudson."

And what became of the plane? It floated down the river. When rescue workers hauled the plane from the river, just half of the tail fin was still above water. The jet had drifted four miles from where it had entered the water.

The Miracle on the Hudson

Directions: Darken the best answer choice.

1. The pilot of U.S. Airways Flight 1549 has the last name
   - (A) Sully.
   - (B) Patterson.
   - (C) Chesley.
   - (D) Sullenberger.

2. The word **altitude** means
   - (A) height above Earth.
   - (B) length of the plane's wings.
   - (C) weight of the plane's cargo.
   - (D) steering ability.

3. What happened third in the life of U.S. Airways Flight 1549's pilot?
   - (A) He learned to fly gliders.
   - (B) He reported a "double bird strike."
   - (C) He made a perfect emergency water landing.
   - (D) He said he had to return to the airport.

4. The Hudson River flows through
   - (A) an airport.
   - (B) New York City.
   - (C) North Carolina.
   - (D) New Jersey.

5. What made this emergency landing so remarkable?
   - (A) No one died.
   - (B) The plane broke into pieces.
   - (C) The governor of New York called it a miracle.
   - (D) Birds had flown into both of the plane's engines.

6. Even after the plane had landed safely, the people aboard still faced the danger of
   - (A) being swept out to sea.
   - (B) getting too cold.
   - (C) bleeding to death.
   - (D) breaking bones.

Answer Sheet

Name: _____

Title: _____

Page: _____

1. Ⓐ   Ⓑ   Ⓒ   Ⓓ

2. Ⓐ   Ⓑ   Ⓒ   Ⓓ

3. Ⓐ   Ⓑ   Ⓒ   Ⓓ

4. Ⓐ   Ⓑ   Ⓒ   Ⓓ

5. Ⓐ   Ⓑ   Ⓒ   Ⓓ

6. Ⓐ   Ⓑ   Ⓒ   Ⓓ

Answer Sheet

Name: _____

Title: _____

Page: _____

1. Ⓐ   Ⓑ   Ⓒ   Ⓓ

2. Ⓐ   Ⓑ   Ⓒ   Ⓓ

3. Ⓐ   Ⓑ   Ⓒ   Ⓓ

4. Ⓐ   Ⓑ   Ⓒ   Ⓓ

5. Ⓐ   Ⓑ   Ⓒ   Ⓓ

6. Ⓐ   Ⓑ   Ⓒ   Ⓓ

Answer Sheet

Name: _____

Title: _____

Page: _____

1. Ⓐ   Ⓑ   Ⓒ   Ⓓ

2. Ⓐ   Ⓑ   Ⓒ   Ⓓ

3. Ⓐ   Ⓑ   Ⓒ   Ⓓ

4. Ⓐ   Ⓑ   Ⓒ   Ⓓ

5. Ⓐ   Ⓑ   Ⓒ   Ⓓ

6. Ⓐ   Ⓑ   Ⓒ   Ⓓ

Answer Sheet

Name: _____

Title: _____

Page: _____

1. Ⓐ   Ⓑ   Ⓒ   Ⓓ

2. Ⓐ   Ⓑ   Ⓒ   Ⓓ

3. Ⓐ   Ⓑ   Ⓒ   Ⓓ

4. Ⓐ   Ⓑ   Ⓒ   Ⓓ

5. Ⓐ   Ⓑ   Ⓒ   Ⓓ

6. Ⓐ   Ⓑ   Ⓒ   Ⓓ

Answer Sheet

Name: _____

page 17
1. Ⓐ Ⓑ Ⓒ Ⓓ
2. Ⓐ Ⓑ Ⓒ Ⓓ
3. Ⓐ Ⓑ Ⓒ Ⓓ
4. Ⓐ Ⓑ Ⓒ Ⓓ
5. Ⓐ Ⓑ Ⓒ Ⓓ
6. Ⓐ Ⓑ Ⓒ Ⓓ

page 37
1. Ⓐ Ⓑ Ⓒ Ⓓ
2. Ⓐ Ⓑ Ⓒ Ⓓ
3. Ⓐ Ⓑ Ⓒ Ⓓ
4. Ⓐ Ⓑ Ⓒ Ⓓ
5. Ⓐ Ⓑ Ⓒ Ⓓ
6. Ⓐ Ⓑ Ⓒ Ⓓ

page 57
1. Ⓐ Ⓑ Ⓒ Ⓓ
2. Ⓐ Ⓑ Ⓒ Ⓓ
3. Ⓐ Ⓑ Ⓒ Ⓓ
4. Ⓐ Ⓑ Ⓒ Ⓓ
5. Ⓐ Ⓑ Ⓒ Ⓓ
6. Ⓐ Ⓑ Ⓒ Ⓓ

page 77
1. Ⓐ Ⓑ Ⓒ Ⓓ
2. Ⓐ Ⓑ Ⓒ Ⓓ
3. Ⓐ Ⓑ Ⓒ Ⓓ
4. Ⓐ Ⓑ Ⓒ Ⓓ
5. Ⓐ Ⓑ Ⓒ Ⓓ
6. Ⓐ Ⓑ Ⓒ Ⓓ

page 21
1. Ⓐ Ⓑ Ⓒ Ⓓ
2. Ⓐ Ⓑ Ⓒ Ⓓ
3. Ⓐ Ⓑ Ⓒ Ⓓ
4. Ⓐ Ⓑ Ⓒ Ⓓ
5. Ⓐ Ⓑ Ⓒ Ⓓ
6. Ⓐ Ⓑ Ⓒ Ⓓ

page 41
1. Ⓐ Ⓑ Ⓒ Ⓓ
2. Ⓐ Ⓑ Ⓒ Ⓓ
3. Ⓐ Ⓑ Ⓒ Ⓓ
4. Ⓐ Ⓑ Ⓒ Ⓓ
5. Ⓐ Ⓑ Ⓒ Ⓓ
6. Ⓐ Ⓑ Ⓒ Ⓓ

page 61
1. Ⓐ Ⓑ Ⓒ Ⓓ
2. Ⓐ Ⓑ Ⓒ Ⓓ
3. Ⓐ Ⓑ Ⓒ Ⓓ
4. Ⓐ Ⓑ Ⓒ Ⓓ
5. Ⓐ Ⓑ Ⓒ Ⓓ
6. Ⓐ Ⓑ Ⓒ Ⓓ

page 81
1. Ⓐ Ⓑ Ⓒ Ⓓ
2. Ⓐ Ⓑ Ⓒ Ⓓ
3. Ⓐ Ⓑ Ⓒ Ⓓ
4. Ⓐ Ⓑ Ⓒ Ⓓ
5. Ⓐ Ⓑ Ⓒ Ⓓ
6. Ⓐ Ⓑ Ⓒ Ⓓ

page 25
1. Ⓐ Ⓑ Ⓒ Ⓓ
2. Ⓐ Ⓑ Ⓒ Ⓓ
3. Ⓐ Ⓑ Ⓒ Ⓓ
4. Ⓐ Ⓑ Ⓒ Ⓓ
5. Ⓐ Ⓑ Ⓒ Ⓓ
6. Ⓐ Ⓑ Ⓒ Ⓓ

page 45
1. Ⓐ Ⓑ Ⓒ Ⓓ
2. Ⓐ Ⓑ Ⓒ Ⓓ
3. Ⓐ Ⓑ Ⓒ Ⓓ
4. Ⓐ Ⓑ Ⓒ Ⓓ
5. Ⓐ Ⓑ Ⓒ Ⓓ
6. Ⓐ Ⓑ Ⓒ Ⓓ

page 65
1. Ⓐ Ⓑ Ⓒ Ⓓ
2. Ⓐ Ⓑ Ⓒ Ⓓ
3. Ⓐ Ⓑ Ⓒ Ⓓ
4. Ⓐ Ⓑ Ⓒ Ⓓ
5. Ⓐ Ⓑ Ⓒ Ⓓ
6. Ⓐ Ⓑ Ⓒ Ⓓ

page 85
1. Ⓐ Ⓑ Ⓒ Ⓓ
2. Ⓐ Ⓑ Ⓒ Ⓓ
3. Ⓐ Ⓑ Ⓒ Ⓓ
4. Ⓐ Ⓑ Ⓒ Ⓓ
5. Ⓐ Ⓑ Ⓒ Ⓓ
6. Ⓐ Ⓑ Ⓒ Ⓓ

page 29
1. Ⓐ Ⓑ Ⓒ Ⓓ
2. Ⓐ Ⓑ Ⓒ Ⓓ
3. Ⓐ Ⓑ Ⓒ Ⓓ
4. Ⓐ Ⓑ Ⓒ Ⓓ
5. Ⓐ Ⓑ Ⓒ Ⓓ
6. Ⓐ Ⓑ Ⓒ Ⓓ

page 49
1. Ⓐ Ⓑ Ⓒ Ⓓ
2. Ⓐ Ⓑ Ⓒ Ⓓ
3. Ⓐ Ⓑ Ⓒ Ⓓ
4. Ⓐ Ⓑ Ⓒ Ⓓ
5. Ⓐ Ⓑ Ⓒ Ⓓ
6. Ⓐ Ⓑ Ⓒ Ⓓ

page 69
1. Ⓐ Ⓑ Ⓒ Ⓓ
2. Ⓐ Ⓑ Ⓒ Ⓓ
3. Ⓐ Ⓑ Ⓒ Ⓓ
4. Ⓐ Ⓑ Ⓒ Ⓓ
5. Ⓐ Ⓑ Ⓒ Ⓓ
6. Ⓐ Ⓑ Ⓒ Ⓓ

page 89
1. Ⓐ Ⓑ Ⓒ Ⓓ
2. Ⓐ Ⓑ Ⓒ Ⓓ
3. Ⓐ Ⓑ Ⓒ Ⓓ
4. Ⓐ Ⓑ Ⓒ Ⓓ
5. Ⓐ Ⓑ Ⓒ Ⓓ
6. Ⓐ Ⓑ Ⓒ Ⓓ

page 33
1. Ⓐ Ⓑ Ⓒ Ⓓ
2. Ⓐ Ⓑ Ⓒ Ⓓ
3. Ⓐ Ⓑ Ⓒ Ⓓ
4. Ⓐ Ⓑ Ⓒ Ⓓ
5. Ⓐ Ⓑ Ⓒ Ⓓ
6. Ⓐ Ⓑ Ⓒ Ⓓ

page 53
1. Ⓐ Ⓑ Ⓒ Ⓓ
2. Ⓐ Ⓑ Ⓒ Ⓓ
3. Ⓐ Ⓑ Ⓒ Ⓓ
4. Ⓐ Ⓑ Ⓒ Ⓓ
5. Ⓐ Ⓑ Ⓒ Ⓓ
6. Ⓐ Ⓑ Ⓒ Ⓓ

page 73
1. Ⓐ Ⓑ Ⓒ Ⓓ
2. Ⓐ Ⓑ Ⓒ Ⓓ
3. Ⓐ Ⓑ Ⓒ Ⓓ
4. Ⓐ Ⓑ Ⓒ Ⓓ
5. Ⓐ Ⓑ Ⓒ Ⓓ
6. Ⓐ Ⓑ Ⓒ Ⓓ

page 93
1. Ⓐ Ⓑ Ⓒ Ⓓ
2. Ⓐ Ⓑ Ⓒ Ⓓ
3. Ⓐ Ⓑ Ⓒ Ⓓ
4. Ⓐ Ⓑ Ⓒ Ⓓ
5. Ⓐ Ⓑ Ⓒ Ⓓ
6. Ⓐ Ⓑ Ⓒ Ⓓ

Answer Key

page 17
1. B
2. A
3. D
4. C
5. B
6. D

page 21
1. A
2. B
3. C
4. D
5. A
6. B

page 25
1. A
2. D
3. A
4. C
5. B
6. D

page 29
1. C
2. A
3. D
4. C
5. B
6. A

page 33
1. D
2. C
3. B
4. A
5. D
6. B

page 37
1. D
2. A
3. B
4. C
5. D
6. A

page 41
1. D
2. A
3. A
4. C
5. B
6. A

page 45
1. A
2. B
3. C
4. D
5. C
6. B

page 49
1. D
2. C
3. B
4. A
5. D
6. B

page 53
1. C
2. D
3. A
4. B
5. C
6. A

page 57
1. B
2. C
3. B
4. A
5. D
6. C

page 61
1. C
2. B
3. A
4. D
5. B
6. D

page 65
1. D
2. B
3. C
4. B
5. A
6. D

page 69
1. B
2. D
3. B
4. C
5. A
6. C

page 73
1. A
2. C
3. D
4. A
5. B
6. A

page 77
1. D
2. A
3. B
4. C
5. B
6. D

page 81
1. A
2. B
3. C
4. D
5. B
6. A

page 85
1. C
2. B
3. D
4. C
5. A
6. D

page 89
1. B
2. A
3. D
4. B
5. A
6. C

page 93
1. D
2. A
3. D
4. B
5. A
6. B